# BREXIT NEGOTIATIONS
## AFTER ARTICLE 50

# BREXIT NEGOTIATIONS AFTER ARTICLE 50

Series Editors: **Alex De Ruyter, Jon Yorke and Haydn Davies, Centre for Brexit Studies, Birmingham City University, UK**

With the vote on 23 June 2016 for the UK to leave the European Union it has become imperative for individuals, business, government and wider society to understand the implications of the referendum result. This series, published in collaboration with the Centre for Brexit Studies at Birmingham City University, UK, examines a broad sweep of topics related to Brexit. It aims to bring together academics from across the disciplines to confront and examine the challenges withdrawal from the EU brings. The series promotes rigorous engagement with the multifaceted aspects of both the 'leave' and 'remain' perspectives in order to enhance understanding of the consequences for the UK, and for its relationship with the wider world, of Brexit, and aims to suggest measures to counter the challenges faced.

## Forthcoming Titles

David Hearne and Alex de Ruyter, *Regional Success after Brexit: The Need for New Measures.*

Arantza Gomez Arana, *Brexit and Gibraltar: The Negotiations of a Historically Contentious Region.*

Stefania Paladini and Ignazio Castellucci, *European Security in a Post-Brexit World.*

# BREXIT NEGOTIATIONS AFTER ARTICLE 50

## Assessing Process, Progress and Impact

EDITED BY

### ALEX DE RUYTER
*Birmingham City University, UK*

AND

### BEVERLEY NIELSEN
*Birmingham City University, UK*

United Kingdom – North America – Japan – India
Malaysia – China

Emerald Publishing Limited
Howard House, Wagon Lane, Bingley BD16 1WA, UK

First edition 2019

**Reprints and permissions service**
Contact: permissions@emeraldinsight.com

**British Library Cataloguing in Publication Data**
A catalogue record for this book is available from the British
Library

ISBN: 978-1-78769-768-3 (Paperback)
ISBN: 978-1-78769-765-2 (E-ISBN)
ISBN: 978-1-78769-767-6 (Epub)

ISOQAR certified
Management System,
awarded to Emerald
for adherence to
Environmental
standard
ISO 14001:2004.

Certificate Number 1985
ISO 14001

INVESTOR IN PEOPLE

# CONTENTS

# LIST OF TABLES AND FIGURES

## Tables

## Figures

# LIST OF CONTRIBUTORS

**Syed Ali** is currently a PhD Student at Aston University and the University of Birmingham. He is researching the readiness of the UK manufacturing sector to transition into industry 4.0 with a focus on the UK automotive sector. Syed holds an MSc in International Business, an MA in Social Science Research Methods from Aston University, and a BSc in Business and Enterprise from the University of Birmingham.

**David Bailey** is Professor of Industrial Strategy at Aston Business School and writes extensively on industrial and regional policy; especially in relation to manufacturing and the auto-industry. David is Chair of the RSA Europe Think-Tank and policy forum and Editor-in-Chief of the *Journal Regional Studies* as well as an Editor of *Policy Studies*, and the *Journal of Industry, Competition and Trade*.

**Sir Mark Boleat** has vast experience in business as well as public and third-sector organisations. These include Director General of the Building Societies Association, the Council of Mortgage Lenders and the Association of British Insurers as well as Chairman of the City of London Policy and Resources Committee.

**Alex de Ruyter** is Professor and Director of the Centre for Brexit Studies at Birmingham City University and has vast experience in research and academic engagement in Brexit and its potential impact on regional economic development, skills and labour market issues. He has published over 50 academic outputs in leading national and international journals.

**A. C. Grayling** is Master of the New College of the Humanities and has written extensively on and edited numerous works of philosophy including biographies of Descartes and William Hazlitt. He is a regular contributor to newspapers, radio and television programmes and is a Fellow of the World Economic Forum at Davos.

**David Hearne** has been a Researcher for the Centre for Brexit Studies since 2017. Previously he worked as an Economist in a regional think tank and his research lies in regional economics and the sectoral and regional impact of Brexit as well as understanding influences on Britain's labour market.

**Kimberley M. Hill** is a Chartered Psychologist, Senior Lecturer and Psychology Programme Leader at the University of Northampton. Kimberley's primary research interests and expertise lie within the areas of social, cognitive psychology and public health. She also sits on a number of national and international professional committees and advisory boards.

**Sir Bernard Jenkin MP** is Conservative MP for Harwich and North Essex and has been Shadow Minister in a number of key departments and select committees. He has served as Chair of the Public Administration and Constitutional Affairs Committee (PACAC since 2015). Bernard is the author of a number of publications on the European Union.

**Di Li** is a Lecturer in Supply Chain Management at Birmingham City University. Her research covers multiple areas within the Supply Chain and Operations Management field, including: Global Supply Network Design (Reshoring and Offshoring, Manufacturing Locations),

Supply Chain in Industry 4.0, Decision Making and Optimization, Sustainability, etc.

**Steven McCabe** is Associate Professor of IDEA and has researched strategy and operations in terms of adoption of TQM and improvement techniques for his PhD. He has written extensively on the subject of management, organisations and politics and has produced numerous papers, chapters for books and three books.

**John Mills** is an Entrepreneur and Economist and Chairman of John Mills Limited (JML). He has extensive experience in local government at regional and national level and was in the late 1980s Deputy Chairman of the London Docklands Development Corporation. He is a long-time 'Eurosceptic' and was Chair as well as Vice-Chair of Vote Leave and Chair of Labour Leave in the 2016 EU referendum.

**Patrick Minford** is a Chair of Applied Economics at Cardiff University and formerly Economic Adviser to HM Treasury's External Division and HM Treasury's Panel of Forecasters. He was Editor of the National Institute Review and Member of Monopolies and Mergers Commission 1990–1996. He was made a C.B.E. for services to economics in 1996.

**Beverley Nielsen** is an Associate Professor/ Executive Director of IDEA (Institute for Design & Economic Acceleration) at Birmingham City University, (BCU). Prior to this she was Director of Employer Engagement and Director of Corporate Affairs at BCU. Before academia she was Director of AGA Rangemaster Plc and MD of Fired Earth. She also worked as Director of CBI West Midlands, gaining lobbying experience as European Policy Advisor in London and Deputy Manager, CBI Brussels.

**Stefania Paladini** is Reader in Economics & Global Security at Birmingham City University. Prior to joining academia in

2008, she worked for the Italian Central Government for fifteen years, seven of which were spent in East Asia as a trade commissioner. She obtained her PhD in International Relations and Security Studies from the City University of Hong Kong.

**Vicky Pryce** is a renowned Economist and Business Consultant and currently sits on the Department of Business, Innovation and Skills' panel monitoring the economy. Previous roles include consulting and being Director General for Economics at the Department for Business, Innovation and Skills and Joint Head of the UK Government Economics Service.

**Sukhwinder Salh** is a Senior Teaching fellow in the Work and Organisational Psychology Department at Aston Business School. She was previously an experienced HR Advisor and an expert on employment law. Whilst she has taught HR for the last 10 years, she also holds a strong generalist background in a number of industries.

**Rebecca Semmens-Wheeler** completed her PhD in 2012 at the University of Sussex, on 'The Contrasting Role of Higher Order Awareness in Hypnosis and Meditation' having previously been a Research Assistant in cognitive neuroscience at Rice University, Texas. She is experienced in designing and delivering learning in a variety of learning environments and is passionate about enhancing pedagogy.

**Shishank Shishank** has a PhD in Operations Management, 'Outsourcing: Decision making during the stages of Design and Engineering', and was previously employed in Project Management an automotive company in India. He is currently examining Brexit and its impact on the automotive and aerospace Industry and understanding the issues for Supply Chain Management.

# INTRODUCTION

*Alex de Ruyter and Beverley Nielsen*

This edited book brings together leading figures from academia, politics and practice to examine the process and impact of impending UK withdrawal from the European Union (EU), some 18 months into Article 50 withdrawal period (at the time of writing). In so doing, we sought to bring together contributors from the diverse fields mentioned to discuss and debate the progress (or lack of) to date since Prime Minister Theresa May enacted Article 50 process to leave the EU on 29 March 2017. This monograph specifically has as its focus two key areas of inquiry: (1) critically examining the dynamics of the withdrawal process from the EU and appraising what opportunities, if any, that 'Brexit' might offer the UK after 29 March 2019, and (2) examining the likely impact of Brexit on key sectors of the UK economy, cognisant of wider social and political issues.

As such, we hope that this edited book will provide a distinct contribution to the considerable literature that has already been produced on Brexit. One of the key distinguishing features of this monograph is that it brings together perspectives from academics and practitioners, both of a 'Remain' and a 'Leave' persuasion. Whilst much material has already been published on the process and likely impact of

Brexit, these publications have largely been of a purely academic contribution operating largely within individual subject areas (politics, law, economics, etc.); and as such, have primarily been from a 'Remain perspective' where Brexit is conceptualised largely in terms of having a forecast negative impact on the UK economy and wider influence in the world, and distinctly lacking in practitioner input.

That is not to in any way discount the consensus of academic opinion in regards to the likely impact of Brexit on the UK economy and society. Rather, what we have felt to be important here, particularly in terms of the contributions from authors of a distinct 'Leave' perspective, namely, Professor Patrick Minford and Sir Bernard Jenkin MP, is to gain insights into the notion that leaving the EU has been driven by a desire to embrace a different regulatory framework than that of the EU. This has been particularly evident with the distinct EU emphasis on 'social partnership' between capital and labour, and the promulgation of law-upholding consumer, worker and environmental rights. That is, for 'Brexiteers', the UK should embrace a more market-oriented deregulatory economy, as purportedly typified by the 'US model' (or otherwise completing the 'Thatcherite Revolution', as it were). For many in this camp, the short-term costs of Brexit are deemed to be worth it for the longer-term gains that realignment of trade and production would offer the UK economy (see Jenkin in this book).

Put in such terms then, Brexit, rather than being a push for 'sovereignty' per se – at least in terms of its leading protagonists – really is more about reasserting the principles of market fundamentalism, or 'completing the Thatcherite revolution' (Hutton, 2017). Andrea Leadsom, one-time leadership aspirant and current Leader of the House voiced these sentiments in no uncertain terms in 2012 when she stated that:

> *I envisage there being absolutely no regulation*
> *whatsoever – no minimum wage, no maternity*
> *or paternity rights, no unfair dismissal rights, no*
> *pension rights – for the smallest companies that are*
> *trying to get off the ground, in order to give them a*
> *chance.*[1]

In a similar vein, Liam Fox, currently Secretary of State for International Trade, writing in the *Financial Times* in 2012[2] stated that:

> *To restore Britain's competitiveness we must*
> *begin by deregulating the labour market. Political*
> *objections must be overridden. It is too difficult*
> *to hire and fire and too expensive to take on new*
> *employees.*

Suffice to say, such sentiments largely did not make it into the popular discourse over Brexit, where the vote has predominantly been interpreted as a reaction against globalisation and 'metropolitan elites' (Pidd, 2016); as a referendum on migration (Golec de Zavala, Guerra & Simão, 2017), or otherwise a revenge of the places that felt 'left behind' (Rodríguez-Pose, 2018). In the chapters that follow, key issues relating to the process and progress of the UK leaving the EU are explored by contributors of varying persuasions and backgrounds (academic, practitioner and politician).

## PART I: BREXIT: PROGRESS, PROCESS AND ISSUES

The first part of the book deals with 'the dynamic of Brexit' – namely those overarching themes raised by the vote and Brexit itself. The opening chapter, by eminent philosopher Professor A. C. Grayling, discusses the constitutional propriety of the referendum and the issues raised by it. Grayling notes that the referendum has exposed the fragility of the UK's constitutional process and the insufficiencies of its constitutional order, going so far as to argue that it has become the 'plaything' of those most able to manipulate it.

The arguments raised as to the inconsistency of the UK's recent use of referenda as a constitutional tool are convincing. It is difficult to understand the rationale for including EU nationals living in Scotland in the 2014 referendum on Scottish independence, but not the 2016 referendum on whether to leave the EU (particularly given that they pay substantial taxes to the British exchequer). Similarly, the 2014 referendum included 16- and 17-year olds, who had not yet reached the age of majority, whereas the latter did not. Grayling then goes on to discuss alleged improprieties in the way the referendum was conducted, arguing that any of these would be sufficient prima facie evidence to declare the results unsafe. Finally, the question of a minimum threshold for major constitutional change is raised. Taken together, Grayling makes a convincing case that the results of the referendum should be treated with caution and not taken as binding upon Parliament.

The book then shifts to consider the economic evidence on Brexit. Professor Patrick Minford is a fierce proponent of free-market economic orthodoxy, placing a high value on theoretical general equilibrium modelling. He is outspoken in his support of Brexit, arguing that it will enable the UK to almost eliminate domestic tariffs and improve welfare. In Chapter 2, the core of Minford's argument is based on his work on trade. Minford differs from many academic economists in entirely eschewing gravity modelling, on the grounds that correlation does not imply causation. However, we note that there is now significant academic literature finding that disintegration of an economic union is followed by a fall in trade intensity (Fidrmuc & Fidrmuc, 2003; Morgenroth, 2017).

Professor Minford focusses on a theoretical approach, so that the results are crucially dependent upon starting assumptions. His assumption that a complete fall back to World Trade Organisation rules will add zero extra trade frictions, for example, will undoubtedly prove a challenging one for many readers in light of the UK Government's no-deal preparations. In this context, the work of Dhingra, Ottaviano, Sampson, and van Reenen (2016), for example, gives very different results and it comes as no surprise to find that there is vigorous disagreement between themselves and Professor Minford (see, e.g., Sampson, Dhingra, Ottaviano, & van Reenen, 2017) on these issues.

Following on from Professor Minford, in Chapter 3, Sir Bernard Jenkin MP forcefully makes the case that Britain should seek a sharp break from the EU. For Jenkin, Brexit must involve two things. First, it should entail an end to the primacy of EU law within the UK and thus a complete break from the role of the Court of Justice of the EU in giving binding interpretations of that law, ruling out membership of the European Economic Area. Secondly, he argues that the UK must be free to negotiate independent trade deals with other potential partners – thus ruling out a customs union with the EU.

Jenkin's perspective contrasts with that of A. C. Grayling, but also with fellow John Mills (Chapter 4) both in outlook and in tone. Jenkin takes particular issue with both the EU's regulatory framework, favouring a low-regulation environment, and the Common External Tariff of the EU's Customs Union. However, the chapter does not explore whether less regulation would have widespread appeal to those 'left behind' communities that appear to have voted so strongly for Brexit. Like Minford, Jenkin favours dramatically lowering tariffs on many products. Nevertheless, many of the hoped-for trade deals could prove difficult to strike and a number of crucial sectors might struggle to take advantage of them due to the probable absence of 'diagonal cumulation'.

In Chapter 4, John Mills, founder of the 'Labour Leave' campaign, provides a short history of the relationship between the British Labour Party and the EU. Drawing on polling data that suggested over one-third of Labour voters voted Leave in 2016 (Ashcroft, 2016), he argues that understanding the rationale behind this is crucial to a thorough understanding of why the UK voted Leave in 2016. Reflecting on the importance of migration to the result, he argues that it is imperative that Labour reacts to worries about pressure on local services and the scale of migration.

Mills is clearly sympathetic to these concerns, noting that many traditional 'Labour working class' voters feel 'left behind' by globalisation and the cosmopolitan internationalism it engendered. Whilst his assertions on the impact of EU migration on service provision and wages are strong, it is true that there appears to be some indication that migration could put some downward pressure on wages for those near the bottom of the wage distribution (Dustmann, Frattini, & Preston, 2013). Nevertheless, Mills' discussion of the likely future options for the Labour party in reacting to the referendum result of 2016 is both interesting and timely. As he concludes, holding the 'Labour coalition' together and charting a course through the waters of Brexit is a daunting challenge.

In Chapter 5, David Hearne, Rebecca Semmens-Wheeler and Kimberley M. Hill deal with the motivating factors behind the Brexit vote from a socioeconomic and psychological perspective. Briefly reviewing some of the key literature from both disciplines, the authors make the case that a holistic understanding of the drivers of the Brexit vote should be multi-disciplinary. Beginning with a brief review of previous social science literature, the authors use a simple econometric model and the referendum results by local authority to investigate the most salient demographic and economic factors that indicate the propensity of a region to vote Leave.

Following this, the authors investigate each of these in turn, noting socio-psychological theories that can begin to explain not just which areas voted for Brexit but why places with certain characteristics may have chosen to vote the way they did. Doing so, the authors argue that this enables them to investigate the validity of various hypotheses around Brexit and bring rigour to a debate that has thus far been characterised by strong assertions around the motivations of those that voted Leave but less evidence. The chapter concludes by noting that there is a strong research agenda moving forward, for both quantitative and qualitative evidence. It is clear that, irrespective of the final outcome, the issues raised by Brexit are not going away and, as such, Brexit will prove fertile grounds for research for some time to come.

In the final section of Part I (Chapter 6), Dr Stefania Paladini examines the issues surrounding the operation of trading outside of a customs union, and the problematic nature of border enforcement in order to prevent the smuggling of contraband items. Using the case of Chinese garlic smuggled under false labelling, Paladini exposes the problems surrounding enforcement at even customs borders such as Norway–Sweden, which is often considered to be a highly efficient operation.

Paladini's work suggests clear implications for any prospective UK–EU trading relationship that results in the UK lying outside the EU Customs Union and Single Market as entailing significant issues in terms of the Northern Ireland border. In the final part of the chapter, Dr Paladini outlines possible options available to the UK. She notes that in contrast to the operation of the Norway–Sweden border, trade between the UK and the rest of the EU is of a different magnitude and hence argues that technological solutions to the Irish border problem probably will not be sufficient.

## PART II: SECTOR-SPECIFIC ISSUES AND
## LIKELY IMPACTS

In Chapter 7, the first of the book's 'sector specific' chapters, Sir Mark Boleat – Chair of the City of London Corporation's Policy and Resources Committee from 2012 to 2017 – outlines the prospective impact of Brexit on the financial services sector. Where Minford and Jenkin see opportunities for the UK's service sector businesses post-Brexit, Boleat argues that, for financial services at least, leaving the EU is likely to prove overwhelmingly negative. In a measured contribution, he outlines how the loss of 'passporting' rights is likely to affect the City's ability to offer services to clients across Europe.

The proposed 'equivalence' measures are considerably weaker and, as noted by Boleat, the process of granting them is often fraught with politics. The chapter notes that a number of major players in the financial services industry are already moving parts of their business into other EU member states in order to ensure that they continue to be able to serve European clients. More generally, firms that wish to do business inside the European Economic Area (EEA) will need to ensure they comply with EU legislation, which the UK will cease to have a role in shaping. The chapter argues that the costs of Brexit for the financial services industry have already been significant – cumulatively running into billions of pounds and are likely to grow further. Finally, the chapter concludes with a rather sober consideration of the potential longer-term ramifications of Brexit.

In Chapter 8, Vicky Pryce, Beverley Nielsen and Steve McCabe discuss the potential impact of Brexit on Small and Medium Enterprises (SMEs) and the wider economy. Taking a broad look at Brexit they note that thus far, evidence suggests that the UK has experienced slower growth since the referendum than would normally be expected. They note the significant impact that uncertainty has had on investment, noting that SMEs are exposed to changes in the business environment via their position in (often long) supply chains. Drawing on survey evidence, they show that small businesses face particular challenges in preparing for Brexit and that access to information is often problematic. Those challenges and difficulties naturally vary by both sector and region with businesses in the manufacturing heartlands of the UK appearing to be particularly exposed. Problems around business support architecture are noted, alongside a failure on the part of government to effectively communicate with smaller firms. In the absence of effective information, many firms are failing to make adequate preparations as they are uncertain as to what the outcome of negotiations is likely to be.

The chapter concludes with concrete proposals derived from extensive survey evidence, suggesting that communication is key. A number of additional proposals around both access to finance and collaboration between the state, private sector and educational establishments (particularly universities) are also put forward. The overarching message is that smaller businesses face unique struggles over Brexit and their views have not been adequately articulated to government.

Finally, in Chapter 9, Di Li, Shishank Shishank, Alex de Ruyter, Syed Ali, David Bailey, David Hearne and Sukhwinder Salh explores the possible impact that Brexit will have on supply chains in the UK automotive industry. Drawing on data collected from interviews with senior managers in the sector, the findings of their research suggest that all current available trading options put up different types of trade barriers for the UK automotive industry, potentially increasing costs and decreasing the UK's attractiveness as a base for automotive manufacturing. The findings of this chapter also suggest that the uncertainty around the UK's trading future with the EU is currently deterring investment into the automotive industry, which will likely have consequences further into the future. They conclude by assessing a wide variety of mitigation strategies open to manufacturers, considering their viability and applicability in each potential scenario.

The book concludes with our thoughts on issues going forward, having noted the findings of the chapter contributors. In so doing, we particularly wish to explore the implications related to the notion of a viable sense of 'Britishness' as a binding identity, or 'Demos' – and also to revisit the notion of economic 'sovereignty' in what is still a highly globalised world. As such, we hope that this book will provide a useful contribution to understanding of the issues raised by the UK's impending departure from the EU.

## NOTES

1. The *Mirror*, 5 July 2016. https://www.mirror.co.uk/news/uk-news/andrea-leadsom-called-minimum-wage-8352620. Accessed on 12 October 2018.

2. The *Financial Times*, 21 February 2012. https://www.ft.com/content/2ee5b8de-5c8d-11e1-8f1f-00144feabdc0. Accessed on 19 October 2018.

## REFERENCES

Ashcroft, M. (2016). *How the United Kingdom voted on Thursday … and why*. Retrieved from https://lordashcroftpolls.com/2016/06/how-the-united-kingdom-voted-and-why/

Dhingra, S., Ottaviano, G., Sampson, T., & van Reenen, J. (2016). *The consequences of Brexit for UK trade and living standards*. Retrieved from http://cep.lse.ac.uk/pubs/download/brexit02.pdf

Dustmann, C., Frattini, T., & Preston, I. (2013). The effect of immigration along the distribution of wages. *The Review of Economic Studies*, *80*(1), 145–173. doi:10.1093/restud/rds019

Fidrmuc, J., & Fidrmuc, J. (2003). Disintegration and trade. *Review of International Economics*, *11*(5), 811–829. doi:10.1046/j.1467-9396.2003.00419.x

Golec de Zavala, A., Guerra, R., & Simão, C. (2017). The relationship between the Brexit vote and individual predictors of prejudice: Collective narcissism, right wing authoritarianism, social dominance orientation. [Original Research]. *Frontiers in Psychology*, *8*(2023) doi:10.3389/fpsyg.2017.02023. Retrieved from https://www.frontiersin.org/article/10.3389/fpsyg.2017.02023. Accessed on September 3, 2018.

Hutton, W. (2017). They're back, as wrong as ever. Enough of Nigel Lawson and his band of 80s ultras. *The Guardian,* October 22. Retrieved from https://www.theguardian.com/commentisfree/2017/oct/21/enough-of-nigel-lawson-and-his-band-of-80s-ultras-brexit. Accessed on September 24, 2018.

Morgenroth, E. (2017). Examining consequences for trade: Integration and disintegration effects. In D. Bailey & L. Budd (Eds.), *The political economy of Brexit* pp. 17–34. Newcastle upon Tyne: Agenda Publishing.

Pidd, H. (2016). Blackpool's Brexit voters revel in 'giving the metropolitan elite a kicking'. *The Guardian*. Retrieved from https://www.theguardian.com/uk-news/2016/jun/27/blackpools-brexit-voters-revel-in-giving-the-metropolitan-elite-a-kicking. Accessed on September 17, 2018.

Rodríguez-Pose, A. (2018). Commentary: The revenge of the places that don't matter (and what to do about it). *Cambridge Journal of Regions, Economy and Society*, rsx024. doi:10.1093/cjres/rsx024. Retrieved from http://dx.doi.org/10.1093/cjres/rsx024

Sampson, T., Dhingra, S., Ottaviano, G., & van Reenen, J. (2017). *Economists for Brexit: A critique*. CEP Brexit Analysis Working Paper No. 6. London: The Centre for Economic Performance.

# PART I

## BREXIT: PROGRESS, PROCESS AND ISSUES

# 1

# BREXIT AND THE QUESTION OF THE UK CONSTITUTION

## A. C. Grayling

These words are being written in the summer of 2018, two years after the referendum on membership of the European Union (EU) which precipitated a 'Brexit' process, and more than a year since notification was given to the EU of the United Kingdom government's intention to take the UK out of the EU.

These words are written within weeks of the UK government submitting proposals to the EU for arrangements to follow the UK's departure, proposals known as 'the Chequers Plan' following a weekend meeting at the Prime Minister's country residence, where agreement among senior members of the government was temporarily reached on what those proposals should be. Within days that consensus ended, along with resignations by cabinet members who objected to it.

The main points of the proposals had been aired on a number of occasions before they were formally presented to the EU, and the EU had already made it plain that they were unacceptable, since they required the EU to compromise central and constitutive features of its structure as a single market within a customs union, with common standards, a number of shared institutions and recourse to a common court of justice for adjudication of disputes and questions about treaty obligations.

Therefore as these words are written, so long after the two events mentioned, there is no agreed plan for what follows departure of the UK from the EU. Complete uncertainty prevails. Serious questions relate to Ireland and Gibraltar. Business is in an anxious state; many companies have already begun to move all or part of their operations to EU countries. The transport industry, and all those industries reliant on just-in-time supply chains, face major questions about their immediate future. Large numbers of skilled EU nationals employed in the National Health Service have departed from the UK, leaving thousands of NHS posts unfilled. Farmers are concerned about the availability of migrant seasonal labour. Evidence, much of it provided by the UK government itself in very belated 'impact studies', of a Brexit's deleterious effects on the UK economy has continued to mount throughout the period in question, showing that warnings given before the 2016 referendum about such effects underestimated the potential harm.[1]

Correlatively, public opinion has moved increasingly against Brexit, as YouGov and other polling results show.[2]

Such is a sketch of the situation as these words are written. To the author of them only one thing has emerged with stark clarity from the EU referendum of 2016 and subsequent events, and only one clear prediction about what will inevitably follow whatever the outcome of the Brexit endeavour. The point of clarity is that the *constitutional* order of the UK is in disarray, and its frailties exposed. The prediction is that this will have to be fully addressed and remedied once circumstances permit. The claim is this: had the relevant features of the

UK's constitution functioned in accordance with established understandings, a Brexit process would not have begun, and the confused and disorganised self-harming situation in which the UK found itself as these words were being written would have been avoided. The fact that this situation arose is evidence that the constitutional order of the state is dysfunctional. The following sets out the considerations in support of this claim.[3]

Certain preliminaries must be noted. One is that, familiarly, the UK has an uncodified constitution, consisting partly in statute and some written conventions (e.g. the Statute of Westminster of 1931 granting Dominion Parliaments a say in matters relating to succession to the crown) and partly in unwritten conventions and understandings. These latter were described by Mill as forming the 'morality' of the constitution, whose force is such that it prevents the use of those powers which, though constitutional, such as the monarch's veto in relation to legislation by Parliament, are inconsistent with what is regarded as acceptable in the political and governmental life of the nation. All authorities on the constitution from Bagehot and Dicey to Jenner and Bogdanor agree on the principal that *Parliament is the sovereign body in the state,* though since accession to the European Economic Community (EEC) in 1973 and subsequent treaties among party states, in which the exercise of some aspects of the UK Parliament's sovereignty are shared with those states; since devolution of various functions of government to Northern Ireland, Scotland and Wales, in which the exercise of some aspects of the UK Parliament's sovereignty in respect of those territories are devolved to the authorities constituted for them; and since the taking effect in 2000 of the Human Rights Act 1998; aspects of sovereignty have been voluntarily self-limited by Parliament, *but not forfeited,* since Parliament has the power to resume its competence in any or all those cases by repealing any or all of those provisions. It therefore remains the supreme sovereign body.[4]

In light of this fundamental principle – Dicey wrote, 'The constitution *is* the sovereignty of Parliament' – it is understood that a referendum does not override the will of Parliament. Referenda are and can only be tests of public opinion, and cannot be binding on Parliament. Members of Parliament (MPs) were reminded of this principle in House of Commons Briefing Paper 07212 §§ 5 and 6 in June 2015, shortly before debate on the EU Referendum Bill began in the House of Commons that month. The principle was reiterated by the Bill's introducer, the Minister for Europe Mr David Lidington, on the floor of the House of Commons on 16 June 2015; he stated, 'the legislation is about holding a vote; it makes no provision for what follows. The referendum is advisory'.[5] Accordingly it was clearly understood that the referendum was a consultative exercise, and neither could nor should – in constitutional terms – be regarded as overriding the competence of Parliament as to what action it should take in light of whatever its result was. In the event, the government chose to regard the outcome as *politically* mandating, because the Prime Minister in office at the time of the referendum had issued a leaflet to all households saying that the government would abide by the outcome.

We note in passing at this juncture that because, in the current state of the UK constitutional order, the executive is drawn from the majority in the dominant part of the legislature, viz. the House of Commons, it is able to act as if it (i.e. the executive) is the sovereign body in the state, because it has a high degree of confidence that it can whip the support of the majority from which it is drawn.[6] However, the conjunction of the referendum's *apparent* outcome (see below) and the *political* decision to treat it as mandating action in accordance with that outcome *independently of and irrespective of* Parliament, raises the question to be discussed below.

Let us first note certain features of the 2016 referendum itself. The franchise for participation in the 2016 EU referendum excluded – after discussion of the matter prior to introduction of the EU Referendum Bill in Parliament – 16 and 17-year olds, expatriate British citizens who had lived abroad for more than a certain number of years, and EU citizens resident in the UK and paying their taxes there. It would seem obvious that all three groups merited inclusion as having a very material interest in the outcome of the vote. In the franchise for the Scottish independence referendum of 2014, 16–17-year-olds had the vote and so did EU citizens resident in Scotland, for precisely this reason.

No threshold was specified for the outcome of the referendum, unlike the 1979 Scottish devolution referendum which required that 40% of the entire electorate should be in favour for any change to take place. The reason given for there being no threshold requirement in the EU referendum, as House of Commons Library Briefing Paper 07212 and the Minister for Europe, on the floor of the House, both explicitly stated, was that the referendum was advisory only, and would not be binding on Parliament or government.

It can be taken for granted that two principal features of an uncodified constitution in which understandings govern the 'morality of the constitution', to use Mill's phrase, are *consistency* and *clarity*. The inconsistency in the formulation of referenda, as exemplified by the differing franchises and the presence in some but not others of threshold requirements, immediately raises questions about their propriety. If the franchise, conditions and consequences of referenda vary from one to the next, there cannot be said to be a clear 'understanding' governing their use in the constitution.

Inconsistency and unclarity is pervasive in the UK constitution. A Trades Union must secure a vote of at least 40% of its entire membership if it wishes to call a strike, otherwise the strike is illegal. A general election cannot be called outside the fixed term of a Parliament unless 66% of the total body of MPs agree. This high bar is set because an election might result in a change of government and therefore a change in the course of the country's affairs. A decision about EU membership has far greater implications for the future of the country's affairs, and yet *no* threshold or supermajority requirement was put in place. The inconsistency here is stark.

In the case of the 2016 EU referendum, although it was inconsistent both with previous referenda and with the reasoning lying behind threshold and supermajority requirements in respect of other constitutional activities, there was at least (temporary) clarity as to its outcome: MPs were expressly advised by Briefing Paper 07212, and then again by the Minister for Europe on the floor of the House, that the referendum was *advisory only, and did not bind Government or Parliament.* Despite this, all three of the following considerations were ignored by the government in the immediate aftermath of the referendum: (a) the fact that no referendum can usurp the sovereignty of Parliament, (b) the fact that the referendum was advisory and non-binding and (c) the fact that Parliament had been expressly so instructed by the minister introducing the Bill in June 2015.

Indeed the government made efforts to act on the *political* mandate it took itself to have, without consulting Parliament at all, by using prerogative powers it claimed to have on the grounds that exiting the EU related to treaty considerations, for which Parliamentary involvement is not required. It will be remembered that the Supreme Court in *R* (on the application of Miller and Dos Santos [Respondents] *v* Secretary of State for Exiting the European Union [Appellant]) 2017 ruled that Parliament had to be consulted; in the event, Parliament debated and voted on a hasty Bill empowering the Prime Minister to trigger Article 50 of the Treaty of Lisbon.

*It did not discuss the outcome of the referendum or the question whether or not the UK should exit the EU.*

This latter is a point of the greatest significance because the outcome of the referendum was that 37% of the electorate given the franchise for the referendum – an electorate which excluded three significant and materially interested constituencies, recall – voted to leave the EU.[7] This outcome is by any standards insufficient to justify a constitutional change so significant as the UK's exiting the EU. There is scarcely any civilised polity in the world where a simple majority, let alone a small one, would permit this: for such a change, a supermajority would be required, of 60% or 66% either of votes cast or the entire electorate. Yet a small minority of actual votes cast, 51.9% to 48.1%, this 'majority' representing 37% of the total electorate, was taken by politicians in favour of Brexit as not merely justifying but mandating the actions they took following the referendum.[8]

Next, in the summer of 2017 Mrs Theresa May, in her capacity as Prime Minister, called a general election, explicitly requesting a mandate from the public for Brexit. This would seem to be an implicit admission that the referendum outcome did not provide such a thing. In the event her Party lost its majority in Parliament, and had to effect a 'confidence and supply' arrangement with a small Northern Ireland party, the Democratic Unionist Party (DUP). Yet having not received the mandate requested, at the head of a minority administration, she continued to pursue a Brexit process.

In the months following the referendum of 2016, it emerged that crimes had been committed by the pro-Brexit Leave campaigns, that there had been overspending by those campaigns, that a number of the claims and promises made by leading proponents of the pro-Brexit campaigns were spurious, misleading or straightforwardly false, and that there is a high likelihood that interference in the campaign from outside the UK had occurred. It would be not merely normal but proper for the outcome of an election or referendum to be regarded as unsafe and therefore to be voided when publicly proven matters such as these come to light. In the UK, no action was taken by the authorities to void the referendum; challenged on the question of the safety of the outcome the government and supporters of the Brexit process chose to ignore these considerations outright.

We turn now to the process itself. It is relevant to recall that the 2016 EU referendum was not necessitated by any crisis in the EU or in the UK's relations with its EU partners; there were no threats or problems arising from EU member-ship, other than those alleged (and alleged for over 40 years of anti-EU activism) by 'Eurosceptics' and certain members of the Conservative Party and UKIP. The referendum was prom-ised as, in fact, an effort by the then leadership of the Con-servative Party to stifle temporarily a long-standing quarrel within that party. During the previous coalition government David Cameron promised a referendum, against the advice of his senior colleagues, to silence the far right of his party. He almost certainly did not expect to win the election of 2015, still less with an outright majority. He had offered the refer-endum as a sop. When he won a majority in the election, he was obliged to honour the promise. Neither he nor anyone else, including the pro-Brexit camp, expected Leave to 'win', so he culpably allowed the Brexit faction to arrange the fran-chise in a way that best suited them – this being the exclusion of 16–17-year-olds (Cameron subsequently said that insist-ing on their inclusion would have made too much trouble with his right wing), expatriates and EU taxpayers in the UK, who between them would have assured a significant Remain majority, a fact the Brexiters well understood.

No one asked the pro-Brexit camp to produce an account of what would follow if a Leave vote won: there were no details, no manifesto, no plan, no roadmap, no assessments of impacts on various sectors of the economy, no explanation of how the gaps in skills, investment, business and trade were to be filled, no account of what arrangement could be reached with our current closest and largest economic partner on our doorstep. There was only one apparent promise – the notorious claim that the EU subvention was to be wholly dedicated to the NHS at the rate of £350,000,000 per week. It is not only the startling fact that voters can be asked to give an imprimatur for a mere negative, without details and undertakings for which accountability can be held, but that the state's constitutional arrangements impose no requirement that votes can be sought in a vacuum. Consider the position of entering a contract: would any court of law enforce a contract in which one of the contracting parties was given no information about what he was contracting for, or in which the undertakings offered by the counterparty were false unfulfillable, and unexplained?

In the absence of any detail on what a Brexit would mean or involve, months after the referendum, months after the Supreme Court case and indeed *after* the debate on Article 50 Bill in the House of Commons, a White Paper on Brexit was published, consisting of a re-edit of some of Prime Minister May's speeches. It does, however, contain two points of interest. One is dealt with in the next section below, concerning the 'sovereignty' not, this time, of Parliament, but of the UK. The other is the statement made in the White Paper's preamble that all 65 million citizens of the UK were 'fully behind Brexit'. This is mentioned because of the constitutional question of 'representation', where 'representation' does not always mean direct electoral representation. The Code of Conduct of MPs, available as House of Commons publications 1474 and 1076, states that MPs are to act in the interests of the state, its peoples and their constituents. In the absence of information about what a Brexit would entail, MPs were in breach of their Code of Conduct in agreeing to a procedure while wholly in the dark as to the consequences for those they 'represent' in both the general and specific senses explicitly required by the Code.

In this connection, it is therefore of relevance to note that 17 million voted for Brexit, 16 million voted against it and 32 million did not vote. The Prime Minister's claim was therefore a form of Newspeak, and involved dismissing the concerns, interests and stated preferences of nearly half the people who voted in the referendum, and of all who could not vote and did not vote. Together with the questionable considerations about the nature and validity of the referendum itself, the EU referendum and its subsequent use by the government is clearly unrepresentative, and therefore constitutionally improper.

The falsity of the claim that 'the country is behind Brexit' is further demonstrated by Scotland, Northern Ireland and Gibraltar; all three voted emphatically to Remain in the EU. Scotland was thereby given renewed justification to seek to leave the UK, and Northern Ireland is faced with an agonising problem over the Good Friday Agreement and its land border with Eire. The particular constitutional poignancy of the Irish border question is that the Good Friday Agreement is a multiparty treaty which works precisely because the UK and the Republic of Ireland are both members of the EU. A unilateral decision to break the terms of the Good Friday Agreement raises questions of international law as well as domestic constitutionality. It also risks lives as well as livelihoods.

The White Paper itself exposes the untruths about sovereignty repeated as part of the Leave campaign.[9] It says in reference to the 'take back control' slogan of the Leave campaign,

> *The sovereignty of Parliament is a fundamental*
> *principle of the UK constitution. Whilst*
> *Parliament has remained sovereign throughout our*
> *membership of the EU, it has not always felt like*
> *that. (section 2.1 Cm 9417)*

To repeat: the UK has always been sovereign, but (says the White Paper) it has '*not always felt like that*'. This section of the White Paper is entitled 'Taking control of our own laws'. There is no mention of the fact that the UK not only agreed to more than 95% of all EU laws but initiated many of them. We read in the White Paper that 'the sovereignty of Parliament is a fundamental principle of the UK constitution' and yet the government treated 37% of a restricted electorate as sovereign, usurping the sovereignty of Parliament by forbidding it to treat an advisory referendum as advisory.

One notes that the White Paper was finished at 4.07 a.m., *after* the debate in the House of Commons on triggering Article 50; publication on the internet always carries a time marker of the moment of publication. White Papers are intended to be information and assessment of options provided *before* debate on a Bill in Parliament. This adds to the serious question about the political legitimacy and constitutional propriety of the post-referendum proceedings.

Let us now summarise the respects in which the EU referendum of 2016, and what has followed upon it in the way of the Brexit process, together contravene the 'morality' of the UK constitution. This is best done by stating what *should* have happened, as justified by precedent and the 'morality of the constitution'.

The franchise for the referendum should have included all those who would be materially affected by its outcome ('all' to be understood as encompassing those persons who, in addition to the adult voting population enfranchised for general elections, can be considered of voting age relevant to the circumstances, as in the 2014 Scottish independence referendum which included those aged 16 years and above). It should have included a threshold requirement, as bearing on a possible major constitutional change. Information about what could be expected in practical terms from both outcomes should have been clearly and fully available to voters so that they were equipped to decide how to use their vote. The referendum's outcome should have been treated as advisory, and should have been specifically debated in Parliament before any action on it was taken, with a view to determining whether Parliament should act on the advice thus given, the debate and any attendant votes being free (unwhipped).

Any one of these steps, each with constitutional precedent and fully within the Mill test as 'constitutionally moral', would have stopped a Brexit from occurring. Inclusion of the three excluded groups of voters would, to a near certainty, have provided a majority for Remain on the day. A threshold of 40% would not have been met. A free debate and free vote in Parliament on the outcome, and on whether to take the advice of 37% of the electorate for a course of action predictably bad for the economy and future of the UK, would to a near certainty not have passed in Parliament.[10] Comprehensive failure of one side of the debate to provide clear information for voters about the consequences of choosing their option would have voided the referendum. Discovery of criminal offences perpetrated by one of the campaigns would have voided the referendum. Discovery of attempted fraud on the voters by false information and false promises ('Turkey joining the EU' and '£350 million a week to the NHS') would have voided the referendum, and would attract the same penalties as does fraud in other circumstances.

Indeed, evidence of crime, fraud and foreign interference, each by itself and certainly in combination, should have rendered the referendum unsafe immediately upon discovery, and voided it. The criminal offences exposed by the Electoral Commission investigation, the misleading information and false promises of the Leave campaigns constituting a fraud on the public, and the connections between the UK and the US instances of foreign interference (the latter being investigated by the US Senate at time of writing), each independently violate the rule of law, and expectations of open and honest dealing in public affairs and matters of public interest and moment.[11] 'Constitutional morality' should not tolerate them.

In short and in sum, the series of constitutional failures from start to finish of the 2016 referendum and its sequelae demonstrate that the constitutional order of the UK has failed in a crucial test. The one clear prediction that can therefore be made is that as the dust settles, one way or the other, on the Brexit episode, this matter will have to be examined.

The UK's constitutional arrangements are Byzantine in their complexity and anomalies. A first practical step has to be to codify those aspects of the constitution which most directly bear on the democracy which confers the people's consent to the legislative and executive branches of government, introducing clarity, consistency and transparency to the procedures by which the people's choices are expressed in elections and referenda, with clear and consistent understanding of what voters must be apprised of in advance, and what they can expect from the various possible outcomes. Constitutional change should never be left to the vagaries of a lazily constructed referendum and political machination alone: that has been the experience of the 2016 EU referendum.

The principle implicit in this last remark is fully present in the provisions of the 2011 EU Act in which those opposed to further integration of the UK in the EU wrote a 'double lock' provision, requiring that any variation of the EU treaties which would entail further integration would require both a referendum and an Act of Parliament before acceptance. The irony, and indeed a further highly questionable manifestation of the *unconstitutional* nature of the 2016 EU referendum and its sequelae, is that this provision of the 2011 Act should require *another* referendum and a *further* Act of Parliament given that the 2016 referendum concerned the question whether the UK should instigate a change to the EU treaties to which it is party. Silently, this 'double lock' was ignored, because in these circumstances it would act *against* the realisation of their wishes. This, perhaps, suffices as a final word on the insufficiencies of the UK constitutional order: it is the plaything of those who know how to manipulate and vary it at will to serve their own interests, precisely the ill attending an uncodified constitution, and correlatively the ill identified by John Locke and Baron de Montesquieu in warning against having no separation of powers between executive and legislature.

## NOTES

1. All these points are in the public domain and can be readily verified.

2. Cumulative polling data: https://whatukthinks.org/eu/questions/if-there-was-a-referendum-on-britains-membership-of-the-eu-how-would-you-vote-2/.

3. Aspects of this argument are discussed further in Grayling (2017). The claim here is that the constitution *as it exists* failed; there is a further argument that the constitution as it exists *is inadequate to purpose*, a fact well illustrated by the Brexit debacle, but not to the point of the argument here.

4. Bagehot (1867), Dicey (1915), Jenner and Bogdanor (2009).

5. Hansard, 16 June 2015.

6. de Montesquieu (1748, Book XI, chapter VI): if 'the executive power should be committed to a certain number of persons, selected from the legislative body, there would be an end of liberty, by reason the two powers would be united' and Locke (1689, chapter 12, § 143) 'because it may be too great a temptation to human frailty, apt to grasp at power, for the same persons, who have the power of making laws, to have also in their hands the power to execute them'.

7. On 23 June 2016, the day of the referendum, 51.9% of votes cast were for the 'Leave' option; this represented 37% of the electorate.

8. One of the Brexit proponents, David Davis, says publicly in Department for Exiting the EU replies to correspondents that the 51.9% referendum majority was 'clear, overwhelming and unarguable'. When the Supreme Court required the government to hold a Parliamentary debate about triggering Article 50, and it voted 8-3 – a 73% majority – Mr Davis said publicly that this majority is 'tenuous'.

9. Cm 9417.

10. It has been common knowledge throughout that a majority of MPs are 'Remainers'.

11. The long-running investigation by Carole Cadwalldr, published in *The Observer* newspaper, and others, establish these links to a high degree of probability, sufficient to render the 2016 referendum outcome unsafe.

## REFERENCES

Bagehot, W. (1867). *The English constitution*. London: Chapman & Hall.

Bogdanor, V. (2009). *The new British constitution*. London: Hart.

Dicey, A. V. (1915). *An introduction to the study of the law of the constitution*. London.

Grayling, A. C. (2017). *Democracy and its crisis*. London: Oneworld Publications.

Locke, J. (1689). *Second treatise on government*.

de Montesquieu, Baron C. (1748). *Spirit of the laws*.

# 2

# THE UK APPROACH TO BREXIT

## Patrick Minford

The British approach to Brexit needs to be understood through the lens of history. We joined the European Economic Community, as it then was, in 1972; and in 1975 there was a referendum on whether we should stay within it, which decided we should. The Thatcher government from 1979 was an enthusiastic backer of the EEC. Yet by 1988, Mrs Thatcher's views had changed radically and in her Bruges speech of that year she vehemently attacked the European Community as it had then become, saying:

> We have not successfully rolled back the frontiers
> of the state in Britain, only to see them re-imposed
> at a European level with a European super-state
> exercising a new dominance from Brussels.

What had changed?

## A BRIEF HISTORY OF OUR EU MEMBERSHIP

We find now that since the advent of the Single Market (SM), European Union (EU) decisions have largely been taken by qualified majority voting (QMV) instead of unanimity. This has meant that the UK, which has been unable to assemble a blocking minority, has been unable to stop a wide variety of measures to which it has been opposed. There are many detailed examples of this including the introduction of labour rights for unions and part-timers, extensive regulations on the financial sector, goods standards that favour dominant continental producers (as with Dyson's annoyance over German firms' successful demands for weak vacuum-cleaner emission tests). However, the two main cases are first the introduction of the Social Chapter and second the introduction of the Euro, both of which were bitterly opposed by the UK governments of both Mrs Thatcher and John Major. Most recently, the Cameron coalition government strongly opposed moves towards political union prompted by the Euro-zone crisis, and insisted that these should be ring-fenced away from the UK at the very least.

'Subsidiarity,' once suggested as a principle for decisions, has turned out to be an empty word. In practice a blocking minority has not existed; and in this respect other countries have also found themselves in the UK's position. With progress towards a 'Federal Union' having become a mantra for the EU's future official plans, these problems of the lack of UK voice threatened to spread from the existing areas of economics – trade policy, regulation and immigration – to wider areas covering foreign policy, defence and internal justice. It became apparent to more and more British citizens from these developments that they were losing democratic control over their laws, institutions and practices. This was the most powerful general motivator of Brexit.

The history by which this situation occurred is instructive. During the 1980s the Thatcher government was enthusiastic about membership of the EU, seeing it as promoting competition, market integration, free trade and free market policies generally. Because of this enthusiasm, the government promoted strongly the idea of the EU SM as an instrument for furthering these free market objectives, with mutual recognition of differing regulative approaches at its centre. M. Delors, the then Commission President, was grateful for this promotion and used it to persuade others in the EU to accept the SM, with its commitment to QMV. However, once it was incorporated in the EU Treaties, M. Delors announced several new initiatives. The first was the Social Market. The second was a drive for uniform regulation, dropping mutual recognition as far as possible. The third was a push for European Monetary Union and the Euro, with accompanying macroeconomic controls to support it.

These initiatives were regarded by the Thatcher government as a betrayal of the objectives they had backed in the SM proposal. Since that time both government and public opinion in the UK has soured towards the EU.

Matters however came to a head because of the massive immigration into the UK from Eastern Europe, permitted under the SM migration freedom. The Blair government in 1997 contributed to the problem by deciding against a seven-year moratorium which was available and adopted by most other countries. A further factor was the UK's non-contributory welfare system, under which any UK citizen is entitled unconditionally to a wide range of tax credits and tax-funded benefits, such as housing benefits, free health care and free education. Because immigrants from the rest of the EU are entitled by law to the same rights as UK citizens – indeed under EU law they are all EU citizens with common rights – they could not be denied this UK taxpayer support. Three million immigrants from Eastern Europe are now in the UK, enjoying these rights. While skilled immigrants contribute amounts in taxes that generally exceed these benefits, unskilled workers (about a third of the total) do not; for them we calculate (Ashton, MacKinnon, & Minford, 2016) that there is approximately a 20% UK taxpayer wage subsidy. Moreover, these workers drive down unskilled wages for UK unskilled workers – an estimate for the Bank of England found that for every 10% rise in immigrant unskilled workers there would be a 2% drop in UK unskilled wages. To make matters worse politically, these costs are highly localised in the poorer areas where unskilled immigrants settle: it is the poor residents of these areas who lose through worse health care and education, higher house prices and lower wages.

Into this explosive mixture intruded the financial crisis and the resulting UK 'austerity' programme. The result was the quick growth of the UK Independence Party (UKIP), to a situation where it was getting some 16% of the national votes, with the Conservatives haemorrhaging support to it. Thus was born David Cameron's promise of a referendum: he hoped it would spike the UKIP attack and yet not be lost to Brexit.

However, his plan went awry, largely because the situation in the UK was not understood elsewhere in the EU. Had it been, and meaningful concessions been offered to Mr Cameron, the government might have won the referendum. But none were and so the government fought the Brexit case without any solution on offer to the problems I have sketched out above. It was forced to fight on the platform of the 'economic disruption' from Brexit, which as we know failed.

While debate continues on whether somehow Brexit can be reversed (e.g. by a second referendum or simply an endless deferral of Article 50 process), the position of both the Conservative government and the Labour opposition is that

Brexit will go ahead; according to most opinion polls there is a popular majority for 'getting on with' Brexit.

Plainly if the economy were to collapse as the Remain side claimed before the referendum, the state of public opinion might change radically. Remainers forecast a recession in the second half of 2016 followed by low growth well below 1% in 2017. This has proved wrong. Growth has continued, even on early ONS estimates that will probably be revised upwards, at close to 2%; the economy is currently at very full employment, with unemployment around 4% and wages starting to grow somewhat faster under tight labour market conditions. Clearly, without Brexit, employment could not have been any fuller; and of course it is far too early for Brexit to have any effect on productivity. Hence, Brexit cannot have had any effect on the level of output. What it has done via the large Brexit devaluation is shift demand away from consumption towards net exports, improving a bad current account deficit that was running at 7% of gross domestic product (GDP) but is now down to 4-5%.

In sum, the current political situation is volatile but the main debate today is on whether there should be a 'hard' or a 'soft' Brexit. To this I now turn.

## WHAT SORT OF BREXIT?

This debate immediately runs up against a problem: 'soft' is not Brexit at all. Therefore, it contradicts the referendum and is therefore on the face of it impossible. 'Hard' or 'Clean' Brexit means that the UK leaves the SM and the Customs Union, and controls migration; it will also pursue Free Trade Agreements (FTAs) with the rest of the world. This was supposed to be government policy. However, the Conservative Party has now been plunged into confusion by Mrs May's

'Chequers proposals', which lie at the extreme 'soft' end of the Brexit spectrum. They envisage the adoption of the EU SM rule-book on goods, together with social and environmental regulation; in practice close to the existing SM regulative set-up. This and the proposed customs arrangement also makes FTAs with the rest of the world impossible on standards and difficult even for tariffs. As the proposals cut across EU SM rules on migration and financial contributions to 'rule upkeep', further UK concessions on these points appear inevitable.

Internal party and Leave voter opposition seems to have spelt the death of these proposals. However, the UK government is continuing to negotiate on them, while Conservative Brexiteers are now advocating a switch to a simple Canada-plus FTA. Now the debate centres around the government's provisional Withdrawal Agreement with the EU which envisages any agreement being delayed to the transition period, subject a 'backstop' in which NI and the UK would be held within EU institutions until agreement is reached, to avoid any UK-Ireland 'hard border'. Parliament has rejected this Withdrawal Agreement and the government is endeavouring to change it with EU agreement. Should no agreement at all be reached either with the EU or within the UK Parliament then trade arrangements will default to conduct under World Trade Organisation (WTO) rules. Other administrative matters alone will then be agreed under Article 50 final agreement.

I now turn to the economic arguments that are relevant to the issues under debate.

## THE ECONOMIC EFFECTS OF BREXIT

Arguments now focus on the long-term effects of Brexit over the next decade and a half. HM Treasury forecast long-term trade disaster with a 7% fall in GDP if the UK left under WTO rules with no EU trade deal. But more recent work shows this is wrong.

The Treasury (and a number of sympathetic other organisations including the LSE trade group, NIESR, OECD and the IMF) used data correlations between trade agreements, trade, FDI and productivity (HM Treasury, 2016) instead of using a Computable General Equilibrium model whose behaviour is based on causal economic theory. These correlations were defended on the grounds that they reflected the role of 'gravity' (i.e. closeness and size affect trade); but plainly correlations do not imply causation and a CGE approach must be used which may have more or less 'gravity effects' in it. In recent work, the Civil Service have produced a joint approach based on a large CGE model along the lines of the GTAP model built at Purdue University, Indiana, and widely used by governments and international institutions to assess trade agreements; in using this model the Civil Service have simply abandoned the methods of the Treasury and its allies. In Cardiff, we have built a smaller and simpler CGE model, in both a 'gravity' and a 'classical' version, for testing whether it can match the UK facts; we find that the gravity version is rejected and the classical fits those facts (Minford & Xu, 2017). However, most telling is that whichever CGE version one uses, Brexit generates similarly strong trade gains.

Besides this original failure of methodology, the wide range of groups finding that the Brexit trade regime damages the UK have all (including a few such as PWC that used a CGE model) made unfavourable policy assumptions about Brexit. The latest Civil Service work based on the GTAP-style CGE model is no exception.

Its Cross-Whitehall Report, which has now been repeatedly leaked to the media and in the summary form of some two dozen PowerPoint slides can be accessed on the House of

Commons website (Civil Service, 2018) assumes that except under the status quo large-scale barriers due to both divergent standards and border hold-ups will emerge between the EU and the UK. It also assumes that we will be unable to reduce trade barriers against other countries much via our proposed FTAs around the world, estimating the gains at only 0.3–0.6% of GDP. Even taking the higher figure this is small indeed. With these assumptions the economy takes a panning, and of course with it virtually all individual sectors as well, including the government and its revenues.

These assumptions are however totally baffling. Standards in the EU and the UK are currently the same and so for either side to maintain they were suddenly incompatible after Brexit would be illegal under WTO rules which outlaw discrimination against foreign suppliers. As standards alter in the future exporters on both sides will adapt in the normal way exporters do all over the world, so again there would be no incompatibility. Furthermore, border hold-ups are also proscribed by WTO rules which mandate a seamless border.

Finally, there is huge scope for our FTAs to reduce the EU trade barriers we inherit: these average 20% on both food and manufactures according to both our own and other research. We know (from Ciuriak et al., 2015) that abolishing these via FTAs with the rest of the world would gain us no less than 4% of GDP according to the GTAP model.

Table 1 summarises the situation for Canada-plus and the WTO option under both the assumptions of this Cross Whitehall Report and also our own work for Economists for Free Trade (EFT).

Hence the Civil Service findings using a GTAP-style model come about using some deeply pessimistic and indefensible assumptions. When reasonable assumptions are put into the GTAP model, it generates good growth from the free trade scenarios of Canada-plus or the WTO option. Indeed the GTAP

Table 1.   Trade Effects under Brexit Scenarios According to
                GTAP-type Model Used by Whitehall.

|  | A: Whitehall Assumptions | | B: EFT Assumptions | |
| --- | --- | --- | --- | --- |
| Trade Barriers expressed as % Tariff Equivalent; Effect on GDP shown as % of GDP in italics | | | | |
|  | Canada-plus | WTO | Canada-plus | WTO |
| Tariffs | – | 4.5 | – | 4.5 |
| *Effect on GDP* | – | *–1.0* | – | *–1.0* |
| New Standards | 16.2 | 20.3 | – | – |
| *Effect on GDP* | *–3.6* | *–4.5* | – | – |
| New Customs | 5.8 | 5.8 | – | – |
| *Effect on GDP* | *–1.3* | *–1.3* | – | – |
| Total Tariff Equivalent (%) | 22.0 | 30.6 | – | 4.5 |
| *Total Effect on GDP (% of GDP)* | *–4.9* | *–6.8* | – | *–1.0* |
| FTAs with rest of world | | | | |
| *Effect on GDP (% of GDP)* | ......+(0.3-)0.6...... | | ......+4.0...... | |
| All Trade Effects on GDP | | | | |
| *(% of GDP)* | *–4.3* | *–6.2* | *+4.0* | *+3.0* |

has examined many such policies over the years, including
Australia's extensive and comparable liberalisation of trade
in the past 30 years where it found a gain in GDP of 5.4%
(Australian Department of Foreign Affairs and Trade, 2017).

In our own Cardiff trade model, we estimate that the net
gains to GDP would be rather larger than this in the case of
the WTO Option: this brings us more gains than Canada-plus
because Brexit comes earlier, the budget contribution falls
away, and the tariff revenues redound to the UK Treasury's
benefit.

On top of such trade policy gains we estimate from our Cardiff modelling that there will be gains from pursuing a degree of UK deregulation compared with highly intrusive EU directives under the SM. Then there are the gains from controlling unskilled migration; and finally the return of our budgetary EU contribution. Together with trade, our work (Minford, 2017a) suggests this will add 0.5% per annum to growth over the next 15 years – around 7% in total to GDP. Consumer prices fall 8% and the living standards of low-income households rise 15%.

## UK NEGOTIATIONS WITH THE EU: POSSIBLE OUTCOMES

We now turn to the question of the likely outcome of the UK negotiations with the EU. We consider in turn three possibilities: the Chequers proposals (a very 'soft' Brexit), Canada-plus and an exit for trade under WTO rules. My focus is on the economics. Plainly the politics is, as already noted, volatile and hard to predict. I will use our Cardiff classical CGE trade model because uniquely we know it matches the facts of UK trade; and I will go into rather more detail than above on our findings. For the Chequers proposals, I shall assume they are not distinguishable from the status quo since they almost entirely replicate current conditions – indeed that is their very aim. In all these cases we assume that EU policies are constant, simply because we have no better assumption.

## EU TRADE NEGOTIATIONS: THE OUTCOME FROM A FULL BREXIT COMPARED WITH A SOFT BREXIT

First, consider the gains the UK can expect from leaving the EU's Customs Union and SM. In the such an event, the EU's protectionism of food and manufactures raises prices for all those products by an average of 20% over the best available prices in the developed world; it could be much more than that compared with best available in the developing world, especially China (Minford, Gupta, Le, Mahambare, & Xu, 2015, chapter 4, gives the basis for these calculations; and see also Berden, Francois, Tamminen, Thelle, & Wymenga, 2009, for direct estimates of non-tariff barriers consistent with these calculations). Eliminating this protection by setting our own tariffs against major world exporters of these products at zero via FTAs would give a big gain from the resulting free trade: calculations indicate that by just eliminating half these barriers consumer prices would fall 8% and GDP be 4% larger (Minford, 2017a).

The EU's SM entails EU regulation across the whole of the UK's economic life-production methods, labour relations, energy market and financial markets – even though only 12% of our GDP is involved in selling to the EU. The rest of the economy sells either in the UK or in the rest of the world. By leaving the SM the UK can in time recalibrate that regulation to suit the UK economy, with gains estimated at around 2% of GDP (see Minford et al., 2015, chapter 2 for the basis). The firms in the 12% who sell to the EU would simply need to meet EU product standards, nothing else. Immigration can be controlled, especially of the unskilled where the UK is obliged under the EU free movement within the SM to give a 20% wage subsidy to EU immigrants through tax credits (net of taxes paid), housing benefits, and benefits in kind such as education and the NHS (see Ashton et al., 2017, for details). This would give another gain which is particularly significant for poorer households whose wages are also depressed by this subsidised competition. These households in fact benefit on the calculations by around a 15% rise in living standards from the trade and immigration changes.

Any UK trade deal with the EU should leave these gains from a 'clean' Brexit intact, on economic grounds alone, leaving aside any political necessity to honour the referendum result. Moreover, for any government at the latter stage of a parliament, it should be a key part of a strategy to boost the economy and demonstrate the future gains to be had from policies that optimistically build on Brexit (Minford, 2017b).

## CANADA-PLUS

By 'Canada' we mean a simple zero reciprocal tariff agreement on goods. Since the UK's product standards are already aligned and since it is to be assumed that rational UK exporters would continue to keep them aligned on their exports to the EU, there can be no 'non-tariff barriers' either way. On this basis there would be 'Full Access' to the SM. Combined with UK FTAs around the world this would ensure that all goods from anywhere reach UK consumers at the most competitive available prices – giving the trade gains of a clean Brexit. Because the UK would be free to regulate its economy as it wished it would also obtain its regulative gains, and also control its borders.

When we turn to services, we can describe Canada-plus as this goods agreement plus mutual recognition of service provision. In other words, UK service providers to the EU and EU ones to the UK would each be free to ply their trade as now.

There continues to be some pressure for the continuation of the SM in financial services in order to retain 'passporting rights' in some form. The Chancellor has tried to accommodate this by indicating that financial services must be part of a final trade deal 'with some sort of enhanced equivalence regime', which will replace existing passporting arrangements.[1] In principle, while this is a desirable outcome, so long as it is implemented in a way that avoids the UK becoming a rule-taker, economically the City will continue to thrive as the world's leading financial centre, deal or no deal. It has been shown that there are various ways to conduct business with EU27 customers from the UK with minimal moves of infrastructure to the EU27 after Brexit (Reynolds, 2017b). Indeed there is no actual necessity for the City to be part of the SM. And while having an 'enhanced equivalence' deal would be preferable this is not absolutely essential either. The sector would also flourish if the UK were its own financial centre, having led the way in framing and shaping much of the international rulebook for financial services.

As the world's leading financial centre, the City sells in all the major markets of the world without receiving any EU protection. In fact, what the EU does and increasingly seeks to oblige its EU member states to do is to put in place a variety of controls for City services, mainly through national regulations of who may sell what in their countries; all that 'passporting' does is to reduce some of the national barriers between member states, making retailing within the EU a bit easier. The estimates suggest only around 9% of City business is even in theory affected by passporting (Economists for Brexit, 2016). In practice, with most firms the passport is principally used for wholesale business and barriers remain in the retail markets. Firms doing retail business inside EU countries typically use local subsidiaries anyway as 'workarounds' for national regulations.

The City will gain from Brexit through the UK reclaiming financial regulation from the EU; and it will expand as free trade brings down its key input prices, especially land, that is, rent as an input cost. It would of course be helpful in the EU trade deal if the EU were to agree to broadbased 'equivalence' under which both sides recognise each other's financial standards as adhering to international over-arching principles established by the world's regulatory bodies (Reynolds, 2017a). This would bring great benefits to the EU in keeping financial markets free within Europe. The EU needs the City which is a significant provider of many financial services.

Should the EU refuse this type of deal and in effect behave in a protectionist self-damaging way, the City would be no worse off in the longer term. The economic model suggests the logic of world market competition will be followed: the City will divert its trade to other world markets, getting the same world prices there as it did before in its EU trade. This simply follows from the logic of world market competition: the EU by restricting its demands for UK financial products in favour of its home producers does not reduce total world demand for these products nor change world supply, so while the UK sells less in the EU, it replaces EU supply in the rest of the world and world prices are the same. Plainly a sensible equivalence deal is preferable as it avoids the short-run costs of such 'trade diversion'; but these are small and quickly got over. To avoid these rather trivial costs by staying in the SM would lose the UK's large and permanent gains from controlling its regulations and its borders described above. I am not including such routine things as airline agreements, tourism or visa arrangements in this 'deal'; these are matters of simple cooperation which need to be concluded for ordinary people all over our continent to carry on their lives. Mostly these agreements are concluded within international bodies (such as International Air Transport Association (IATA) in the case of airlines). Some such as visas involve bilateral action by governments. In some cases (such as hotel provision) firms simply need to adopt country standards in shaping their products.

What we notice from this analysis is that the EU gains from access to UK service provision, especially the City. In general, the EU Commission has pushed for freer trade in services consistently, attempting to reduce national protection of services not always successfully. On a variety of indicators, the UK erects few barriers to foreign service provision already. The EU would not wish to erect barriers on top of those already in place from EU-27 national governments. It follows that the EU will gain from continuing the existing situation in services, while the UK will be content to carry on as now. This gives us the 'plus' in Canada-plus.


## WHAT IF THERE WAS NO TRADE DEAL WITH THE EU?

Here it is important to use a proper trade model. As noted in Minford and Xu (2017) the classical model passes the test of matching the facts of UK trade, while the gravity model is rejected. Accordingly we will use the classical model.

Under no deal, but one where the UK pursues its planned policy outside the SM and Customs Union, of creating free trade by signing agreements with the non-EU world, the key effect is to lower UK prices of food and manufactures and create competition inside the UK economy with these new prices. Plainly with an EU free trade deal with no reciprocal tariffs and other trade barriers, EU goods would also arrive free of any duty or other hindrance in the UK and would also compete with these world prices; we can assume that in order to preserve their sales their prices would fall in line; otherwise they would lose all their sales, which we assume they continue, in order to contribute to their overheads.

For UK producers selling in the EU home competition would force their EU prices to equality with world prices: were one UK producer to get more others would divert output to their market, driving prices into line.

Suppose instead there was no deal and this consisted of existing tariffs being levied mutually by both sides (remembering there would be no non-tariff barriers because these would be discriminatory, given all export products on both sides satisfy product standards and can be assumed to continue to do so by virtue of industries' own self-interest.) Then the same logic would apply for pricing by EU producers selling in the UK: they would have to match the new competition, so that their UK prices would remain the same as with a deal. Similarly, for UK producers selling into the EU; home competition would force them to match home competition with their EU prices. Therefore, EU producers would now have to absorb the UK tariff; and EU consumers would have to pay the EU tariff on top of the invariant UK price. Hence the tariffs on both sides would be paid by the EU, the UK tariffs by EU producers to the UK Treasury, the EU tariffs by EU consumers; of course, the EU would receive the tariff revenue from its own consumers, making its overall loss equal to the UK tariff revenue – estimated at approximately £13 billion (Protts, 2016).

On top of this the WTO option would mean that there would be no UK financial settlement and no transition period. The EU would be short of some £28 billion over the rest of its budgetary septennial to 2020 (with the UK paying two years' contributions at about £14 billion a year); it would also lose the longer-term contribution to net liabilities, reported to be worth another £10 billion or so. Also, because its Customs Union with the UK would stop immediately, it would lose two years' worth of the terms of trade gain its producers make on its balance of trade surplus with the UK – estimated at around £18 billion a year: so two years' worth of that would be another £36 billion one-off loss. Some have suggested that the EU Commission would take a narrow view and welcome receiving the tariff revenue on UK exports, even though this would be being paid for by EU consumers; however, this is estimated at a mere £5 billion per year (Protts, 2016), less than half the loss of the UK contribution. It does not alter the grim picture of no trade deal for the EU.

From the UK viewpoint paying no financial settlement would be a gain, avoiding the need to pay some £38 billion. So with no transition period, free trade, own-regulation and own-border-control would come two years earlier, bringing forward that long-term gain at roughly 6% of GDP excluding the budgetary transfer, that would amount to some 12% of GDP; assuming that it would otherwise arrive in 2030, bringing it forward to 2028, when discounted at 3% a year, means it would be worth around an extra one-off gain of 9% of GDP, around £180 billion. It would also gain that tariff revenue paid by the EU producers to the UK Treasury, of £13 billion p.a.; which again, discounted, would be worth some £433 billion.

It would seem that overall the breakdown of talks would be positive for the UK to the tune of a one-off gain of £38 billion on the EU budget, plus £180 billion from bringing forward the non-budgetary Brexit gains, plus £433 billion from EU tariff revenue, some £651 billion in all. For the EU it would mean a one-off loss of £38 billion in financial settlement, plus another one-off loss of £36 billion in terms of trade gain, plus the permanent loss due to paying UK tariff revenue of some £13 billion a year which at a 3% discount rate would be equivalent to a one-off loss of £433 billion. So plus £651 billion for the UK versus minus £507 billion for the EU: it could not be more open and shut who least wants a breakdown. For the UK, a breakdown would be a short-term nuisance but a substantial economic gain; for the EU it is both a short-term nuisance and a substantial economic loss.

From an economic viewpoint, this WTO-based scenario with no trade deal is damaging to the EU and the EU should react to this possibility by adopting a Canada-plus agreement. It seems highly likely that the UK would agree to this, once it was plain that the Chequers proposals were not viable. While as we have seen the UK does better with a WTO-based exit than under Canada-plus, it would prefer the latter on general grounds of neighbourly cooperation. Nevertheless, noncooperative politics may yet trump these economic considerations.

## CONCLUSIONS: THE POST-BREXIT WORLD WILL BE A BETTER WORLD

The analysis here has suggested that of the three Brexit outcomes discussed here, which between them appear to cover the spectrum of possibilities, the Chequers proposals would, if agreed so as to satisfy the EU, essentially represent no change from the status quo. Politically it would be worse because we would have no input into the EU's future rule-making; it could also be economically worse if by losing this input new rules are more damaging to us. In this exercise we have assumed there would be no such future changes. But insofar as there are changes that damage the UK's interests, the status quo with which our alternatives are compared is that much worse.

These two alternatives, Canada-plus or the WTO-based exit, would both involve a 'clean' or 'full' Brexit as I use the terms here: opponents would also describe them as a 'hard' Brexit.

This chapter has argued that either of these 'full Brexit' outcomes would promote economic gains not merely for the UK but also internationally. The UK will sign FTAs around the world – with countries including US, China, South Korea, Australia and New Zealand. These FTAs will cause a drop in world protection and lead to a general search among participating countries for better world trade relations.

The UK and the EU will continue to have open capital markets as now, benefiting from free flows of capital including Foreign Direct Investment.

The UK will regulate pragmatically in areas that are important for its future growth, especially for new technologies, such as bio-technology in food and medicine. It will create good environment for its vital financial industries. It will look again at regulation in the area of energy policy and climate change, and seek a less costly approach.

In immigration, the UK will move to a skills-based policy, which is even-handed between immigrants from all over the world.

As a result of faster growth there will be a Brexit Dividend for the UK public finances, which we estimate at £60 billion p.a. by 2025. This can be used to deliver tax cuts and meet public spending priorities, ending 'austerity'. Lower income households will benefit particularly.

The EU will gain too, though less so in the WTO-based case. It will have on its doorstep a country pursuing free market policies. Its loss of one-fifth of its protected market in food and manufactures will force its producers to become more productive.

It will lose 11% of its budget and hence need to make cuts in subsidy programmes and find a way of raising new general taxation that can buy off vested interests without giving protection, the EU's internal curse.

With exit now seen to be a viable alternative, resistance to centralisation will increase across the EU; this will strengthen the EU as an institution permitting more regulatory competition and devolution of power.

Brexit will therefore strengthen free markets not just in the UK but also the EU and the rest of the world. It will inaugurate an important supply-side revolution.

## NOTE

1.  https://www.bloomberg.com/news/articles/2018-01-25/hammond-says-he-s-very-happy-with-where-pound-is-at-the-moment

## REFERENCES

Ashton, P., MacKinnon, N., & Minford, P. (2016). *The economics of unskilled immigration*. London. Retrieved from http://www.economistsforfreetrade.com/the-economics-of-unskilled-immigration/

Australian Department of Foreign Affairs and Trade (2017). *Australian trade liberalisation: Analysis of trade impacts*. Retrieved from https://dfat.gov.au/about-us/publications/trade-investment/Documents/cie-report-trade-liberalisation.pdf

Berden, K., Francois, J., Tamminen, S., Thelle, M., & Wymenga, P. (2016). Non-tariff measures in EU-US trade and investment: An economic analysis. Final report ECORYS (in Breinlich et al. (2016) [Table of ntbs on p 123]).

Breinlich, H., Dhingra, S., Ottaviano, G., Sampson, T., Van Reenen, J., & Wadsworth, J. (2016). *BREXIT 2016: Policy analysis from the Centre for Economic Performance*. London (p. 154).

Ciuriak, D., & Jingliang, X., Ciuriak, N., Dadkhah, A., Lysenko, D., & Badri Narayanan, G. (2015). *The trade-related impact of a UK exit from the EU SM* – A research report prepared for Open Europe by Ciuriak Consulting. Retrieved from http://ssrn.com/abstract=2620718

Civil Service. (2018). *EU exit analysis – A cross-Whitehall briefing*. PowerPoint slides (p. 27). Retrieved from

https://www.parliament.uk/documents/commons-committees/
Exiting-the-European-Union/17-19/Cross-Whitehall-briefing/
EU-Exit-Analysis-Cross-Whitehall-Briefing.pdf

Economists for Brexit. (2016, December). *A brief on the City after Brexit: Written evidence to the International Trade Committee*. Retrieved from https://www.economistsforfreetrade.com/wpcontent/uploads/2017/08/ABriefontheCityAfterBrexit-WrittenEvidencetoIntlTradeCom....pdf

HM Treasury. (2016). HM Treasury analysis: The long-term economic impact of EU membership and the alternatives. Ref: ISBN 978-1-4741-3089-9, PU1908, Cm 9250PDF, 8.97MB (206 pages).

Minford, P., Gupta, S., Le, V., Mahambare, V., & Xu, Y. (2015, December). *Should Britain leave the EU? An economic analysis of a troubled relationship* (2nd ed., p. 197). Cheltenham: Edward Elgar Publishing.

Minford, P., & Xu, Y. (2017). Classical or gravity: Which model best matches the UK facts? *Open Economies Review*, forthcoming. Retrieved from https://link.springer.com/content/pdf/10.1007%2Fs11079-017-9470-z.pdf

Minford, P. (2017a). *From project fear to project prosperity: An introduction*. Retrieved from https://www.economistsforfreetrade.com/wp-content/uploads/2017/08/From-Project-Fear-to-Project-Prosperity-An-Introduction-15-Aug-17-2.pdf

Minford, P. (2017b). *On behalf of economists for free trade, 'A budget for Brexit – Economic report.'* Retrieved from https://www.economistsforfreetrade.com/wp-content/uploads/2017/11/EFT-Budget-for-Brexit-14.11.17.pdf

Protts, J. (2016). *Potential post-Brexit tariff costs for EU–UK trade. Briefing note: October 2016, Civitas.*

Retrieved from http://www.civitas.org.uk/reports_articles/
potential-post-brexit-tariff-costs-for-eu-uk-trade/

Reynolds, B. (2017a). *A template for enhanced equivalence:
Creating a lasting relationship for financial services between
the EU and the UK*. London: Politeia.

Reynolds, B. (2017b). *The art of no deal: How best to
navigate Brexit for financial services*. London: Politeia.

# 3

# THE UK ECONOMY AND TRADE POST-BREXIT

*Sir Bernard Jenkin MP*

## INTRODUCTION

The United Kingdom's vote to leave the European Union (EU) was neither a vote to be poorer, nor was it a vote to turn its back on the rest of the world. Evidence shows the motivating factors behind the vote were a desire to return sovereignty to British institutions (Ashcroft, 2016), while also representing a rejection of the European political project (Bulmer & Quaglia, 2018).

The EU's approach to the rejection of further integration, combined with the rebalancing necessitated by the formation of the Euro (Frieden, 2015), meant the direction of the EU has become increasingly unacceptable to many in the UK. The vote to leave was fundamentally a manifestation of the desire of the British people to be governed by their own institutions (Ashcroft, 2016).

Forecasts of recession, mass joblessness and rampant inflation (HM Government, 2016) have not come to pass. The UK is currently (at the time of writing) experiencing record levels of employment (The Department for Work and Pensions, 2018).

In order to make the most of the advantages from Brexit – namely to use the control of trade policy and regulations to tailor the country to a changing world – it is crucial that any post-Brexit trade deal with the EU does not present barriers to those advantages. In the view of the author, a preferred future relationship would be based on a Canada-style free trade agreement with zero tariffs on goods and services, as well as bilateral military and security cooper-ation. However, the UK should not fear exiting without a negotiated agreement: the World Trade Organisation (WTO)-terms option.

Taking a long-term view, any short-term disruption could be more than rewarded by recapturing control of the UK's tariff schedules, trade policy and goods and services regula-tions (Minford, Gupta, Le, Mahambare, & Xu, 2015). The share of UK exports which go to the EU has been declining in the past decade, and share of exports to non-EU countries has significantly increased (Office for National Statistics, 2017). Ultimately, the UK's economy could be strengthened as a result of Brexit, as long as the freedom to increase competi-tiveness and trade with other countries is retained and used (Minford, 2017). This represents a significant opportunity to make the UK an international leader in trade, with the natu-ral consequences of greater growth and economic security for this country's residents for years to come.

## WHAT MOTIVATED THE VOTE? CONFIDENCE IN THE ECONOMY AND PROSPECTS OF THE UK

The claim has been made that the vote was driven by xenophobia, a fear of the modern world and by a return of isolationism (Golec de Zavala, Guerra, & Simão, 2017). This was not the message of the official Leave campaign, of which the author was a director. Vote Leave did not argue for isolationism or intolerance. These may be the views of a vociferous minority, but polling undertaken at the time of the referendum found that for nearly half of Leave voters, the biggest single reason for wanting to leave the EU was

> *The principle that decisions about the UK should be taken in the UK.*[1] *(Ashcroft, 2016)*

Notwithstanding the demographics of those who voted Leave, the debate is about taking back control: about democratic self-government and the UK's right to make its own laws and choose how it engages with other countries on matters such as trade.

The formation of the Euro was always a political project and it transformed the EU. It made integration an imperative to prevent the Euro from failing (De Grauwe, 2013). Moreover, it runs the risk of side-lining the UK as decisions are taken to protect Eurozone integrity on the basis of a qualified majority within the EU. After the 2008 banking crisis, there followed the Eurozone crisis, whose consequences can be seen today, as the people of Greece are forced by their bailout conditions to find a 3.5% budget surplus until 2022 and run a 2.2% surplus until 2060.[2]

## HOW THE ECONOMY HAS FARED SINCE BREXIT

To understand where a post-Brexit economic policy will take the UK, it is important to understand where it is today. In the period since the referendum result, the UK's economy has defied the predictions of economic crisis and collapse (HM Government, 2016).

Indeed, the then Chancellor George Osborne's said

> *A vote to leave would cause an immediate and*
> *profound economic shock creating instability and*
> *uncertainty which would be compounded by the*
> *complex and interdependent negotiations that*
> *would follow.*
>
> *The central conclusion of the analysis is that the*
> *effect of this profound shock would be to push*
> *the UK into recession and lead to a sharp rise in*
> *unemployment.*[3]

In the 'severe shock' scenario, the impact of the vote to Leave, house prices were predicted to fall by 18%. Unemployment would rise by 820,000. Consumer Price Index (CPI) would be increased from 2016 levels by 2.7% and the deficit would increase by £39 billion (HM Government, 2016). Having now experienced the two-year period for which the report made immediate predictions, it is clear that these predictions have not come to pass. Following the referendum result, the UK's economy has continued to grow and unemployment has fallen further (The Department for Work and Pensions, 2018), despite the uncertainty caused by the protracted negotiations.

Far from more than unemployment rising between 520,000 and 820,000, constituting a rise between 1.6% and 2.4%, unemployment has fallen from 4.9% in March 2016 to 4.0% in June this year – a level not seen since the 1970s.[4,5]

Moreover, the UK's growth to July was recently upgraded to 0.6%.[6] The predicted shock to public finances also did not materialise: 2018–2019 borrowing is approximately 40% down on the same period in the previous financial year.[7]

## WHAT BREXIT MEANS FOR THE UK'S RELATIONSHIP WITH THE EU

The vote to Leave has a number of clear policy consequences. Departing from the EU should mean repatriating control of all UK laws, an end to the jurisdiction of the Court of Justice of the EU, ending massive contributions to the EU's budget, ending free movement of people and regaining the freedom to strike trade deals across the world.

In order to fulfil this mandate, it is necessary for the UK to leave the Single Market and the Customs Union. The 'four freedoms'[8] are a central tenet of the Single Market, meaning that some common regulatory standards and free movement of labour are core elements.

Leaving the Customs Union is crucial for trade policy considerations and after doing so the UK exchequer will receive those customs duties that the UK chooses to levy.[9] Furthermore, the Customs Union's defining features are centralised European control of tariff rates, quotas and tariff-rate quotas for goods entering the Customs Union from outside.

## OUTCOMES OF POSSIBLE BREXIT PLANS

This chapter will largely assume that the UK's final relationship with the EU is based on an extended version of the Comprehensive Economic Trade Agreement (CETA) recently signed between the EU and Canada, the details of which are explained at greater length below.

### Canada

A Canada-style free trade agreement was originally offered to the UK by Donald Tusk[10] at the March European Council this year:

> *I propose that we aim for a trade agreement covering*
> *all sectors and with zero tariffs on goods. Like other*
> *free trade agreements, it should address services.*[11]

Such an agreement would cover all sectors including services. It would maintain zero tariffs and quotas between the UK and the EU. Extensions to the agreement could also cover enhanced security and defence cooperation. This proposal, which has now been fully explained by the Institute of Economic Affairs in their recent paper, *Plan A Plus*, is also known as 'Canada +++'.[12]

Unlike other proposals, the UK would be free of any constraints imposed by the EU Customs Union, trading with the EU under a similar customs procedure as it does with every other non-EU country in the world. It would also be free of the Court of Justice of the EU and all entanglement with the Single Market, meaning the repatriation of the making and interpretation of all law to the UK. The UK could be free to conclude FTAs with countries around the world, without any hindrance from being tied to the EU's regulatory regime.

## WTO Terms

The third option is to leave the EU without a negotiated agreement, and therefore trade on the terms determined by the WTO. The UK's trading relationship with the EU would be largely on the same terms that we currently trade with states with which we have no preferential trading agreement (e.g. China or the USA). The FTAs which the EU has concluded with third countries would hopefully be grandfathered to become UK-third country FTAs, although it is possible that subsequent negotiations would enable an improvement on the terms the EU has agreed on behalf of the 28 present EU members (although granted, there are issue of diagonal cumulation to consider).

## DOMESTIC ECONOMIC ADVANTAGES OF BREXIT

As long as any trade deal reached between the UK and the EU does not prevent the UK from concluding FTAs with other countries, the economic benefits from Brexit would be significantly derived from finding new markets for British products, lowering household prices due to lowering tariffs and the benefits of free trade, while also tailoring the UK goods and services regulations to increase competitiveness (Minford, 2017; Minford et al., 2015).

The EU's Common External Tariff has always been detrimental to the UK's interest because the European Economic Community, the precursor to the modern EU, had a Customs Union which was designed and built before the UK's entry in 1973. Some of the high food tariffs continue to be very damaging to the UK as a net food importing nation (Minford, 2016, 2017; Minford et al., 2015). British consumers pay 100% of the elevated prices for food inside the EU's tariff walls, but only part of the benefit goes to British farmers. Much of the revenue raised from tariffs on food imports and paid for by UK consumers goes to farmers in other EU countries.

The EU's high tariff areas can be seen from Table 1.

The EU's external tariffs mean that UK consumers pay, while producers in other EU countries benefit. This can most easily be understood with products not made or grown in the UK, for example, oranges which face a high tariff which was increased to 16% in October 2016.[13] There is no production of oranges in the UK and therefore no domestic industry to protect. At the moment, therefore, the British consumer can buy Spanish oranges tariff-free, but must pay 16% tariffs

Table 1.   Average EU Tariff by Product.

| Average EU Tariff by Product Type (%) | |
| --- | --- |
| Animal products | 15.7 |
| Dairy products | 35.4 |
| Fruit vegetables and plants | 10.5 |
| Coffee and tea | 6.1 |
| Cereals and preparations | 12.8 |
| Oilseeds, fats and oils | 5.6 |
| Sugars and confectionery | 23.6 |
| Beverages and tobacco | 19.6 |
| Cotton | 0.0 |
| Other agricultural products | 3.6 |
| Fish and fish products | 12.0 |
| Minerals and metals | 2.0 |
| Petroleum | 2.5 |
| Chemicals | 4.5 |
| Wood, paper, etc. | 0.9 |
| Textiles | 6.5 |
| Clothing | 11.5 |
| Leather, footwear, etc. | 4.1 |
| Non-electrical machinery | 1.9 |
| Electrical machinery | 2.8 |
| Transport equipment | 4.3 |
| Other manufactures | 2.6 |

*Source*: WTO World Tariff Profiles (2017, p. 82)

on oranges imported from the rest of the world.[14] The overall effect of this protectionism is that Spanish and other EU
orange growers are free to raise their prices, set their price at
the 116% of the global trading price of an orange. In effect,
UK consumers must pay 16% more for their oranges than if
oranges were let into the UK at world prices.

Leaving the EU, and freeing the UK's import markets from the Common External Tariff, could lower prices for consumers in the UK's market for products on which tariffs are imposed, as long as any subsequent tariffs were lower than the equivalent Common External Tariff. Other than tariffs, the rules of the Single Market for goods also raise prices inside the EU above world levels due to the imposition of non-tariff barriers (NTBs) against imports of many goods from outside the EU. One estimate of the impact of NTBs on price levels is that the combined effect of the EU's tariff and NTBs on imports of goods from the rest of the world is to raise prices of food and manufactured goods inside the EU to 20% above world prices on average (Minford, 2017).[15]

UK consumers are therefore paying on average 20% above world prices for goods which they buy from the EU27. By the same logic, UK exporters also reap a 20% premium above world prices for the goods which they export to the EU27. And if the UK were a major exporter of goods, then it would be the case that it would benefit from this policy. However, in 2017, the United Kingdom exported £164 billion of goods to the EU27 and imported £259 billion, giving a deficit of £95 billion in goods trade (Office for National Statistics, 2017).[16]

If the average price level of goods traded inside the EU single market is 20% above world price levels, then the *net* over-price paid by UK consumers (i.e. after offsetting the benefit to UK exporters of goods to the EU27 of receiving a similar overprice) is £16 billion per year. This high figure is paid for by UK consumers paying the higher prices.

This is an approximate calculation and the 20% estimate may well be too high. Equally, the net overprice paid by UK consumers on goods imports from the EU27 may be significantly greater than the £16 billion figure estimated above.[17] Whatever the precise level, it is clear that UK consumers are significantly overpaying for the £295 billion of goods bought from the EU27 each year. These goods could be bought more cheaply on world markets if the present wall of tariff barriers and NTBs against imports from the rest of the world is relaxed once we leave the EU. These NTBs relaxed would not be those related to product or agricultural safety and, in any case, relaxing the tariffs imposed on goods brought into the UK do not make the import of unsafe goods any more or less likely.

Leaked estimates from the European Commission suggest that seven unspecified European regulations are costing British businesses billions of Euros each year.[18] Moreover, repatriating control of a country's regulations has significant long-term effects. Studies suggest that returning sovereignty to nations has long-term benefits for economic growth:

> there is the related possibility of considerable gains from self-rule and sovereignty, not only in the political but also an economic sense .... The long-term growth model suggests a maximum positive impact from these two growth sources of some 1.2 percentage points per year. But applying just half of this potential would increase annual average growth to 2050 to 2.8%, or 2.4% in per capita terms – a similar rate achieved by the UK economy during the 1950–1973 and 1995–2007 booms.[19]

The specific advantages of a WTO-Terms exit from the EU are also not to be dismissed. Under those conditions, the legal advice accepted by the House of Lords Constitution Committee made clear that there is no obligation to make the £39 billion payment that would be part of the Withdrawal Agreement.[20] In that case, this could be used to ameliorate the effects of short-term disruption of leaving the EU without an agreement. Furthermore, the automatic imposition of WTO-level tariffs on the UK's substantial imports from the EU would provide a further boost to public finances, though the government may well decide to reduce or to abolish some tariffs to protect consumers from higher prices on some commodities.

## THE UK'S RELATIONSHIP WITH THE REST OF THE WORLD

Leaving the EU will have obvious negative effects for UK access to the EU's markets. However, once outside the EU, the UK will be able to develop new trading relationships. These opportunities include the possibility of joining the Comprehensive and Progressive Agreement for Trans-Pacific Partnership and a comprehensive free trade agreement with the US, including financial services.

A comprehensive trade deal with the US, which includes services, would give UK firms better access to its population of over 320 million and the world's largest single economy.[21] With the UK accounting for 7% of world service exports and the USA 15%, they would together account for over a fifth of the global total: a market of huge significance.[22]

The 11 TPP countries have a population of almost the same as the EU at 500 million people and represent a market of more than $10 trillion in economic output, which is 13.5% of the global total.[23] The Commonwealth has a population of 2.3 billion people, many of whose countries are growing faster than the EU.

Outside the EU, there are new opportunities to develop trade across Asia and Africa, where future growth is also expected to be most rapid. The EU has historically represented the UK's trade interests poorly for two key reasons:

1.  Sometimes regulatory change within the EU is slow. Similarly, the CETA trade deal with Canada took more than seven years to negotiate, and was delayed by a single Belgian region.[24] Negotiations between the EU and Japan are still ongoing, and have taken at least six years. [25]

2.  EU negotiators have had to take account of 28 states' interests, which will quite naturally be varied. Trade deals negotiated directly by the UK can therefore be made more tailored.

Restoring the UK's freedom to negotiate and sign trade deals could not only speed up trade negotiation, but will free the UK from needing to negotiate in the interests of the remaining 27 members. The Department for International Trade is already pursuing these opportunities and countries like Australia and Brazil have already expressed an interest in concluding free trade agreements with the UK.[26] The USA continues to express an interest in concluding a 'big trade deal' with the UK.

Domestic government policies could have a much bigger impact on economic performance than whether the UK is inside or outside a customs union with the EU. It is significant that the UK's departure from the EU will give it greater flexibility, more responsibility and more accountability over how we manage our economy as the UK will regain:

*   control over its tariff schedules;

*   the ability to set regulatory standards and decide how they should be applied;

*   the unencumbered freedom to set VAT rates; and

*   freedom from the Common Agricultural Policy and Common Fisheries Policy.

## CONCLUSION

As this chapter has demonstrated, leaving the EU could bring significant benefits both to UK businesses and to UK consumers.

These benefits arise from the greater regulatory freedom that the UK would enjoy, and from no longer being a part of the Single Market or the Customs Union. This is not about 'lowering standards' but about having the flexibility and freedom to ensure that standards are applied in the most appropriate way. In some areas, such as in respect of the environment, marine stewardship, food safety, food labelling and animal welfare, the UK will wish to apply much higher standards than the EU allows.

The capacity to lower tariffs for goods that are not produced by vulnerable domestic industries would have the effect of lowering goods prices in the UK market. Control over the UK's regulations, both for goods and services, will lead to lower prices for consumers as well as greater competitiveness for UK-based businesses.

These benefits will be retained in the event of a WTO-terms Brexit, that is, without a negotiated withdrawal agreement. There are also additional benefits to leaving the EU on such terms, such as the availability of the £39 billion payment currently part of the Withdrawal Agreement.

Leaving the EU in such a fashion as to take advantage of these is not just a policy choice – it is the fulfilment of the democratic mandate issued by the people of the UK on 23 June 2016. The decision to leave the EU was not due to short-sighted protectionism or a desire for the UK to be closed off from the rest of the world. Rather, the vote was to see a UK with ambitions wider than just the country's closest neighbours, and to create new relationships of mutual benefit with countries around the world.

## NOTES

1. Lord Ashcroft Polls: *How the United Kingdom voted on Thursday ... and why.* http://lordashcroftpolls.com/2016/06/how-the-united-kingdom-voted-and-why/. Accessed on 04 March 2018.

2. FT: *Eurozone hails Greece's exit from bailout as end of crisis.* https://www.ft.com/content/aeb930e0-a475-11e8-926a-7342fe5e173f. Accessed on 20 August 2018.

3. HM Government: *HM treasury analysis: The immediate economic impact of leaving the EU.* https://assets.publishing.service.gov.uk/government/uploads/system/uploads/attachment_data/file/524967/hm_treasury_analysis_the_immediate_economic_impact_of_leaving_the_eu_web.pdf. Accessed on 16 May 2018.

4. Op Cit: HM Government: *HM treasury risk analysis.*

5. ONS: *UK Labour Market: September 2018.* https://www.ons.gov.uk/employmentandlabourmarket/peopleinwork/employmentandemployeetypes/bulletins/uklabourmarket/september2018#main-points-for-may-to-july-2018.

6. Guardian: *UK GDP growth lifted by hot weather and World Cup.* https://www.theguardian.com/business/2018/sep/10/uk-gdp-growth-july-retail-construction. Accessed on 10 September 2018.

7. FT: *Record July surplus spells relief for Hammond on NHS pledges.* https://www.ft.com/content/00d197ac-a51e-11e8-8ecf-a7ae1beff35b.

8. Freedom of movement for goods, services, capital and labour.

9. OBR: *Customs Duties assumptions post-Brexit.* http://obr.uk/box/customs-duties-assumptions-post-brexit/. Accessed on March 2017.

10. Although under this proposal, Northern Ireland would remain within the EU regulatory orbit.

11. European Council Press Release: *Statement by President Donald Tusk on the draft guidelines on the framework for the future relationship with the UK.* http://www.consilium.europa.eu/en/press/press-releases/2018/03/07/statement-by-president-donald-

tusk-on-the-draft-guidelines-on-the-framework-for-the-future-relationship-with-the-uk/. Accessed on 07 March 2018.

12. Institute for Economic Affairs: *Plan A+: Creating a prosperous post-Brexit UK*. https://iea.org.uk/publications/plan-a-creating-a-prosperous-post-brexit-uk/. Accessed on 24 September 2018.

13. Brexit Central: *New 16% import tariffs on oranges show why we must leave the Customs Union*. https://brexitcentral.com/dan-lewis-new-16-import-tariffs-oranges-show-must-leave-customs-union/. Accessed on 29 November 2016.

14. With the exception of certain countries, most notably South Africa, with which the EU has Free Trade Agreements. The government's policy is that these existing EU FTAs should be 'novated' so they continue to apply to the UK after exit and note that South Africa has agreed to this.

15. *Economists for free trade: From project fear to project prosperity*. https://www.economistsforfreetrade.com/wp-content/uploads/2017/08/From-Project-Fear-to-Project-Prosperity-An-Introduction-15-Aug-17-2.pdf. Accessed on August 2017.

16. ONS: *Pink Book 2018* section 9, table 9.4. https://www.ons.gov.uk/economy/nationalaccounts/balanceofpayments/datasets/9geographicalbreakdownofthecurrentaccountthepinkbook2016.

17. A study published by Civitas calculated that if the EU's Common External Tariff were notionally applied to UK exports to the EU27, £5.2 billion would be payable, whereas on the same assumption £12.9 billion tariffs would be payable on EU27 imports into the UK. The big disparity in the figures is because (1) the EU27 export more goods to the UK than vice versa; but also (2) the EU27's exports to the UK are much more heavily concentrated in high tariff sectors. http://www.civitas.org.uk/reports_articles/potential-post-brexit-tariff-costs-for-eu-uk-trade/.

18. Politico: *Brussels: May's Brexit plan would save UK businesses billions*. https://www.politico.eu/article/european-commission-chequers-theresa-may-brexit-plan-would-save-uk-business-billions/. Accessed on 27 August 2018.

19. FT|IE|Corporate Learning Alliance: *Looking on the bright side: UK growth after Brexit*. https://www.ftiecla.com/2017/04/26/

looking-on-the-bright-side-uk-growth-after-brexit/. Accessed on 26 April 2017.

20. House of Lords European Union Committee: *Brexit and the EU budget*. https://publications.parliament.uk/pa/ld201617/ldselect/ldeucom/125/125.pdf. Accessed on 02 March 2017.

21. IMF website – data. http://www.imf.org/external/pubs/ft/weo/2017/02/weodata/weorept.aspx?pr.x=57&pr.y=10&sy=2015&ey=2022&scsm=1&ssd=1&sort=country&ds=.&br=1&c=924%2C111&s=NGDPD%2CPPPGDP&grp=0&a. Accessed on 09 March 2018.

22. ONS 2017 *The Pink Book*, chapter 9.14. https://www.ons.gov.uk/economy/nationalaccounts/balanceofpayments/datasets/9geographicalbreakdownofthecurrentaccountthepinkbook2016. Accessed on 09 March 2018.

23. Australian Government website – Department for Foreign Affairs and Trade – Trans-Pacific Partnership Agreement – TPP-11 Market Snapshot. http://dfat.gov.au/trade/agreements/tpp/outcomes-documents/Pages/outcomes-documents.aspx. Accessed on 09 March 2018.

24. BBC: *Ceta: EU and Canada sign long-delayed free trade deal*. https://www.bbc.co.uk/news/world-europe-37814884. Accessed on 30 October, 2016.

25. BBC: *EU and Japan reach trade deal*. https://www.bbc.co.uk/news/business-40520218. Accessed on 06 July 2018.

26. See: Interview with Australia's High Commissioner, Alexander Downer on the Today Programme, 12 February 2018. http://www.bbc.co.uk/news/av/uk-43030034/australia-says-yes-to-post-brexit-free-trade-agreement-with-the-uk. Accessed on 09 March 2018 and Wallace (2017).

## REFERENCES

Ashcroft, M. (2016). *How the United Kingdom voted on Thursday … and why*. Retrieved from https://lordashcroftpolls.com/2016/06/how-the-united-kingdom-voted-and-why/

Bulmer, S., & Quaglia, L. (2018). The politics and economics of Brexit. *Journal of European Public Policy, 25*(8), 1089–1098. doi:10.1080/13501763.2018.1467957

De Grauwe, P. (2013). *Design failures in the Eurozone: Can they be fixed?* Lex Paper No. 57, 40. doi:https://dx.doi.org/10.2139/ssrn.2215762

Frieden, J. (2015). The political economy of adjustment and rebalancing. *Journal of International Money and Finance, 52*, 4–14. doi:https://doi.org/10.1016/j.jimonfin.2014.11.010

Golec de Zavala, A., Guerra, R., & Simão, C. (2017). The relationship between the Brexit Vote and individual predictors of prejudice: Collective narcissism, right wing authoritarianism, social dominance orientation. *Frontiers in Psychology, 8*(2023). doi:10.3389/fpsyg.2017.02023

HM Government. (2016). *HM Treasury analysis: The immediate economic impact of leaving the EU*. Retrieved from https://assets.publishing.service.gov.uk/government/uploads/system/uploads/attachment_data/file/524967/hm_treasury_analysis_the_immediate_economic_impact_of_leaving_the_eu_web.pdf

Minford, P. (2016). *Understanding UK trade agreements with the EU and other countries*. Retrieved from http://patrickminford.net/wp/E2016_1.pdf

Minford, P. (2017). From project fear to project prosperity. In *Economists for Free Trade*. https://www.economistsforfreetrade.com/wp-content/uploads/2017/08/From-Project-Fear-to-Project-Prosperity-An-Introduction-15-Aug-17-2.pdf.

Minford, P., Gupta, S., Le, V. P., Mahambare, V., & Xu, Y. (2015). *Should Britain leave the EU? An economic analysis of a troubled relationship* (2nd ed.). Cheltenham: Edward Elgar Publishing.

Office for National Statistics. (2017). *UK balance of payments, The Pink Book: 2017*. Retrieved from https://www.ons.gov.uk/economy/nationalaccounts/balanceofpayments/datasets/9geographicalbreakdownofthecurrentaccountthepinkbook2016. Accessed on March 14, 2018

The Department for Work and Pensions. (2018). *Press release: Employment rate at new record high*. Retrieved from https://www.gov.uk/government/news/employment-rate-at-new-record-high

Wallace, T. (2017). *Brazilian finance minister attempts to woo the UK with free trade offer. The Telegraph*. Retrieved from https://www.telegraph.co.uk/business/2017/09/30/brazilian-finance-minister-attempts-woo-uk-free-trade-offer/. Accessed on March 09, 2018.

# 4

# THE BRITISH LABOUR PARTY'S ATTITUDE TOWARDS THE EU – A BRIEF HISTORY

## *John Mills*

The Labour Party's attitude to what is now the European Union (EU) has a long, chequered and inconsistent history. It is important to understand where Labour has come from to appreciate where it now is and where it may be going to be as the Brexit negotiations move to a climax.

## BACKGROUND

The recent story begins in the immediate post-World War II period when the original architects of what eventually came to be the EU began to rebuild trust and institutions between the nations of Europe which had fought themselves to destruction during the years running up to 1945. The first concrete manifestation of their plans was the creation of the European Coal and Steel Community, established in 1952.[1] The UK was asked to join but declined to do so. Reflecting Winston Churchill's speech at Zurich in 1946, when he advocated the UK 'being with Europe but not of it' and 'linked but not impaired',[2] similar views were subsequently reflected in statements by Ernest Bevin, Labour's Foreign Secretary,[3] and by Prime Minister Clement Attlee, the Labour Prime Minister.[4]

The UK therefore took little part in the negotiations which led up to the Messina Conference, held in 1955,[5] at which the seeds of what became the European Economic Community (EEC), or the Common Market were planted. The UK was invited to send a delegate but declined to become involved. An abortive attempt to establish a free trade area in Western Europe was sponsored by the UK, along similar lines to the subsequent European Free Trade Association (EFTA) arrangements, but the main continental leaders were not interested in a purely economic approach.[6] From the beginning, the EEC objective was to establish a supra-national political entity. Britain therefore stood on the side-lines, with little dissent from the UK Labour ranks. In 1957, the Treaty of Rome was signed and the integration which led to the EU began to take effect.[7]

The 1950s and 1960s were a period when the countries in Western Europe did exceptionally well in terms of economic growth, averaging some 4% per annum cumulatively – a much better record than in the UK where the economy was expanding at little more than half the continental rate.[8] At the same time, decolonisation left the UK without an Empire and the role in the world which the country had enjoyed for two centuries, while the Suez debacle showed how much weaker the UK had become. The loss of confidence thus engendered led to the original application – rebuffed at the instigation of General de Gaulle – by the Conservative government of the time to join what was still the EEC in 1961, followed by a second abortive application in 1967.[9] Finally, the Heath government, elected in 1970, succeeded in winning round our continental neighbours, and the UK joined the EEC at the beginning of 1973.[10] While Edward Heath and many Conservatives at the time regarded this as a triumph, this was not a view shared widely in the Labour Party, which opposed the UK joining the EEC on the terms which had been negotiated. It was in 1962 that Hugh Gaitskell, the Labour leader, told the Labour Party Conference that joining the EEC would 'mean the end of 1,000 years of history',[11] and there had been little change in Labour's attitude to the EEC since then.

When Labour won both the general elections held in 1974, the party was severely split on how best to proceed. It was then agreed that attempts should be made to change and improve the terms of membership agreed by the Heath government on the footing that there would then be a referendum to determine whether the UK should stay in the UK or leave. The resulting changes were small but sufficient for Harold Wilson, the Labour Prime Minister, to claim that they tipped the balance in favour of continuing membership. The subsequent 1975 referendum split the Labour Party roughly down the middle as the referendum campaigning got under way. Everyone from the cabinet downwards was allowed to campaign for what they thought should be the outcome. An array of Labour heavyweights, including Peter Shore, Barbara Castle, Michael Foot, Tony Benn and Jack Jones, the leader of the then very powerful Transport and General Workers Union, campaigned for leaving.[12]

While roughly half of the Labour Party and its supporters voted for no longer remaining in the EEC, the split among the Conservatives was much more strongly tilted towards staying in. With roughly 80% support from the right, the outcome of the referendum June 1975[13] was a two-thirds majority for continued membership. This did not stop continuing concern among a large section of the Labour Party about this outcome, however, and if anything, the Party became more

Eurosceptic over the next few years, culminating in a resolution passed by the Labour Party Conference in 1982, calling once more for the UK to leave the EEC.[14]

During the late 1980s, however, the tide began to turn. With Margaret Thatcher in power, Jacques Delors made a powerful speech at the 1988 Trades Union Conference, promising a social component to the integration taking place within the EU which won over many trades union leaders.[15] At the same time, Neil Kinnock, the newly elected Leader of the Labour Party – despite his previous scepticism – swung round to supporting the UK's EEC membership, the overall result being that the Labour Party over the coming years became more and more Europhile – while exactly the opposite was happening among Conservatives. During the battles over the treaties building closer EU integration – at Maastricht, Nice and Amsterdam – it was the Conservatives who made the running in opposing this direction of travel.[16]

The 2008 financial crash and the faltering UK growth rate, lacklustre productivity growth and stagnant incomes, led to increased discontent, much of it focussed on the EU, generating the rise of UKIP – the UK Independence Party. Initially, support for UKIP came mostly from Conservatives, causing David Cameron, the Conservative Prime Minister from 2010, to promise to hold a referendum on the UK's continuing membership of the EU.[17] With a large majority of Labour MPs and party members strongly in favour of continued membership and with Conservatives split roughly down the middle, he was reasonably confident that those supporting Remain would win. Perhaps he might have been right if the EU had been a little more accommodating on migration and other issues as negotiations with European leaders running up to the referendum took place, but this was not to be. The result of the referendum was a small but decisive majority for Leave.[18]

## THE 2016 EU REFERENDUM

Crucially, according to an extensive poll carried out and published by Lord Ashcroft shortly after the referendum, 37% of those who had voted Labour in the 2015 general election plumped for Leave in 2016.[19] Although the Labour Party generally was highly Europhile, the same could not be said for many traditional Labour voters, particularly in Wales, the Midlands and the North of England. This is a crucial part of the Labour story.

Why did not far short of 40% of the 2015 Labour voters cast their votes for Leave? There has been a marked tendency among Remain supporters, particularly those relatively insulated from areas of the country outside the M25, to attribute Leave voting to those who did so being ill-informed and bigoted. It was true that voting Leave was heavily concentrated among relatively low social status sections of the population, many of whom had comparatively poor levels of academic attainment. It does not follow from this however, that Leave Labour voters were unaware of what they were voting for. Of course, all democratic decisions are taken by people with less than full knowledge of every aspect of the implications of the votes they cast. In the case of the referendum, however, the choice to be made was relatively simple: Leave or Remain. Although the implications were complex the choice to be made was relatively straightforward. Why did so significant a proportion of Labour supporters vote Leave?

Some of the Leave Labour voters were in the Far Left camp, regarding the EU as a neoliberal capitalist club which would inhibit the implementation of traditional socialist policies, a view enjoying a considerable amount of sympathy from Jeremy Corbyn and some of his close associates with long track-records of Eurosceptic voting patterns. Others were aware in reasonable detail of the standard Eurosceptic arguments about border control, the net cost of membership, legislative hegemony, the disadvantages of the Common Agricultural Policy and the Common Fisheries Policy and the implications of membership on the UK's ability to strike trade deals on its own account. It is hard to believe, however, that any of these reasons for voting Leave were paramount among Labour leaning voters, and all the evidence suggests that they were not. Much more important were simpler emotional arguments of which far the most important were about taking back control and controlling immigration. The poll by Lord Ashcroft, referred to above, indicated that the most persuasive arguments for Leave for about 50% of Leave voters were around control, about one-third to do with immigration, with all the other arguments making up no more than one-sixth of the remaining reasons for voting.[20]

Taking back control was undoubtedly a reaction not just against the EU, although the EU's remoteness, bureaucracy and the poor image of it portrayed in much of the popular press must have been an important factor. Much of the 'control' vote was a bitter reaction against years of austerity, stagnant real wages and cuts in public services, deindustrialisation and privation, for which the EU was only to a limited extent directly responsible. The problem was that the EU symbolised for many people the whole phenomenon of the metropolitan elite losing touch with non-metropolitan culture and values. The EU, in particular, was associated with the cosmopolitanism and internationalism which globalisation had generated, which was regarded very positively by many Remain supporters but which for many people on the other side represented the reasons why their wages and job prospects had stagnated or diminished. The strength of feeling thus engendered was powerful enough to overcome all the pressure put on them to vote Remain. One of the more iconic events at the time of the referendum was that voters in

Sunderland, in which Nissan has a large and very successful car plant, voted strongly to Leave despite dire warnings from the Nissan management about what the consequences of a vote for Leave – so far not fully realised, though with threats still outstanding – might be.[21]

Although immigration and border control, shading into race-prejudice and bigotry, were often cited by Remainers as being the most powerful reason for most Leave voters casting their ballots the way they did, the evidence for this is not well founded. What certainly is the case is that many Leave supporters believed – with ample justification – that the rise in population in the UK, fuelled by EU migration was putting a large amount of pressure on resources such as schools and hospitals and that the large-scale influx of able and willing immigrants from Eastern Europe, willing to work for much lower wages than those indigenous UK residents expected to earn, was putting significant downward pressure on wage levels. Although the evidence for the latter is not completely clear-cut, there must have been some of this happening especially in some areas such as those involving large amounts of fruit-picking.[22] A strong desire – part of the general urge to exercise more control over their lives – to see some reasonable constraints put on immigration especially from Eastern Europe was not, therefore, in the vast majority of cases motivated by racism but by legitimate concerns over local facilities and wages – important issues which many felt had been badly neglected – not least by the Labour Party itself.

Reflecting the views of most Labour MPs and Party members, Labour decided as an organisation to campaign for Remain and this was a policy pursued with varying degrees of vigour and unity by the constituency Labour parties as well as by most Labour MPs.[23] Some were more enthusiastic than others, with the less convinced including Jeremy Corbyn, who at one point during the referendum campaign described the

EU as meriting a score of no more than 7 out of 10.[24] There were also a small number of Labour MPs, notably Kate Hoey, Kelvin Hopkins, Graham Stringer and Frank Field who campaigned strongly on the Leave side. Graham Stringer was on the Board of Vote Leave throughout the campaign.

In the end, it was the Labour vote which, as much as anything else, swung the referendum result the way it eventually went. Both Remain and Leave organisations detected a marked softening in support for Remain and a rising level of backing for Leave among Labour voters during the weeks running up to the vote on 23 June 2016, as the Labour Leave messages, particularly on control and immigration, cut home.[25] When the results were announced, nearly 70% of all the parliamentary seats held by Labour had Leave majorities.[26]

## RECENT DEVELOPMENT

Since the referendum, Labour has agonised over how to respond. All but a handful of Labour MPs had voted Remain, many of them with constituencies with significant and sometimes large Leave majorities. The dilemma which all these Remain Labour MPs faced was that a clear democratic decision had been taken with which most of them disagreed. The issue which all these MPs needed to resolve was how to square the referendum vote with what they thought should be done in consequence. Should they accept the referendum result and consent to the UK leaving the EU, quite possibly on comprehensive terms, outside the Single Market and the Customs Union as well as out of the EU's political structure? If not, should they try to retain as much of the relationship which the UK enjoyed with the EU on the Single Market and the Customs Union, even if nominally the UK was to leave the EU? Or was it better to campaign to reverse the referendum result altogether by supporting campaigning whose objective was to secure the UK's continuing membership of the EU?

The situation was further confused by the election of Jeremy Corbyn as Leader of the Party in September 2015 on the crest of a huge recruitment wave as hundreds of thousands of new people joined the Party, a large proportion of them being Momentum supporters.[27] Generally, these people favoured Remain, although the new Labour leadership continued to have reservations. The strong support for Remain among the Labour Party's new members was, however, concentrated, in London and a few university towns. This was strikingly brought out in the general election which took place in June 2017 as the Conservative Prime Minister, Theresa May, attempted unsuccessfully to increase her party's parliamentary majority. Labour's vote went up by almost 4 million, increasing as a share of the total vote from 29% to 40%, but this only brought Labour a net gain of four seats. Ominously, 130 Labour MPs, mostly with seats in Wales, the Midlands and the North of England, saw their share of the vote declining. This happened despite the fact that the Labour Party, as well as the Conservatives, had declared in their election manifestos that they proposed to follow through the referendum result by negotiating the UK's departure from the EU. These commitments undoubtedly helped to squeeze the UKIP vote, whose support slumped to less than 2% of the total votes cast.[28]

The 2016 general election had a critical impact on the way Brexit negotiations were going. The Prime Minister had set out in a speech at Lancaster House – in January 2017 before the general election – a reasonably clear path. The UK was going to leave the Single Market and the Customs Union and effectively negotiate a free trade deal similar, but hopefully more comprehensive, than the Comprehensive Economic and Trade Agreement (CETA) deal just negotiated between the EU and Canada.[29] The composition of the new 2017 parliament, with no overall majority for the Conservatives who had to be buttressed by the Northern Irish Democratic Unionist Party, however, contained no majority for any such an outcome. As the Conservative government, even before the general election, had conceded to EU proposals that citizenship, the Irish border and money should be discussed and substantially agreed before serious discussions on trade had even begun, the government was already batting on a sticky wicket, with the situation worsened by deep divisions among Conservative MPs. The result was a messy compromise to enable trade talks to begin, agreed in December 2017, which parked the Irish Border problem but left the EU with the whip hand in dealing with the implications of what had been agreed.[30]

The Labour responses to these developments fell uneasily into various responses. An opposition's job is to oppose and the instability the Conservative administration provided an added fillip to Labour determination to try to bring down the government and to force another general election. This was not likely to be a successful tactic, however, as Conservative MPs were determined to avoid another general election if they possibly could. Doubts over the Prime Minister's leadership and Brexit policy, however divisive they might be, have continued not to tip dissident Conservative MPs into supporting a vote of confidence which would bring the government down. This left Labour in a position where its major tactic was to criticise and condemn government policy on the basis that it had been mishandled. Sir Keir Starmer, with the Labour Brexit brief, summarised Labour's stance by enumerating six points which Labour said had to be recognised in any outcome which was going to secure Labour support. This included adherence to a statement originally made by David Davis MP, then the chief government Brexit negotiator, that Brexit negotiations would lead to the UK enjoying 'exactly the same benefits' as we have at the moment.[31] Since this was certain never to be achievable in practice in any foreseeable circumstances short of the UK remaining fully in the EU, this left Labour with a reason to vote down more or less any proposals which the government brought forward.

Over the summer of 2018, the Conservative voting arithmetic in the House of Commons broke down into perhaps a maximum of 80 Conservative MPs who much preferred a Clean Brexit, Canada type deal on the one hand, and a substantial dissident Conservative group, perhaps 20 strong, who, like the vast majority of Labour MPs, were reluctant to see the UK giving up the advantages of the Single Market and the Customs Union. In these circumstances, the Prime Minster had no majority in Parliament for neither a CETA model Canadian deal nor going back on the referendum result by staying in the Single Market and the Customs Union. This led to the Chequers proposals, so called because they were endorsed by the cabinet at a meeting a Chequers on 6 July 2018, although instigating the resignations of David Davis and Boris Johnson shortly afterwards. These proposals were then sold to everyone, including the EU, as the only realistic basis on which an agreement with the EU could be secured. They were met by predicable hostility across the political spectrum and by the EU but remain in play because, in the last analysis, they may provide the framework for the only kind of deal which will get through Parliament and be acceptable to the EU. The very narrow votes in favour of the government's stance, some of them only achieved because of the support of the same small number of Labour MPs who have always been in favour of a Clean Brexit – some now in trouble with their constituency Labour parties – shows how tight the votes in Parliament in future may well be.[32]

## THE FUTURE

As of February 2019, it is far from clear what the outcome of the Brexit negotiations is going to be. It may be that the EU will become a good deal more flexible than it has been up to now, allowing some version of the Chequers deal to secure a majority in the House of Commons. It is possible that Chequers may shade into being something similar to the Norwegian situation in the European Economic Area, although the path to this position is not simple, especially with the short time available. It may be that negotiations will break down, leading to the UK leaving the EU with no deal on trade in place, thus reverting back to World Trade Organisation (WTO) terms, possibly with some kind of free trade arrangement in place with the EU. It is also possible that nothing will be finally settled by 29 March 2019, with decisions deferred to a later date while existing arrangements continue what will no doubt be described as being on a temporary basis – although the provisional has a habit of being difficult then to change into something else. What is Labour likely to do and which of these options is likely to find favour with the Parliamentary Labour Party and with its membership?

It seems probable that when the chips are down, Labour may be tempted to support a Chequers based deal, if, in the light of implacable opposition from the hard-line European Reform Group, this is the only way of getting anything through Parliament. As an outcome of this sort is, however, likely to be viewed unfavourably by a large section of the electorate, including many Leave-orientated Labour supporters in the critical marginal seas in Wales, the Midlands and the North of England. This may therefore be a difficult decision for Labour MPs to take. If the vote for Chequers is then lost, it looks as though the choice is then going to be between both the UK and the EU recognising that either there will, by default, be a WTO approach, with or without free trade, or there will be a fudge without any concrete parliamentary approval as all final decisions are put on hold and deferred to the future.

This process is very likely to be complicated by the With-drawal Agreement which was scheduled to come before Parliament either during the autumn of 2018 or early in 2019. This will be a legally binding document in which the EU would like to see an irrevocable commitment by the UK to pay to the EU the £39 billion proposed by the Prime Minister in her September 2017 Florence speech.[33] Rather more than half this sum covers budgetary commitments agreed by the UK for the EU 2014–2020 budgetary period and which there is general consensus that we have a moral if not a legal obligation to honour. The reminder, although vital to the EU to deal with budgetary commitments which the EU would otherwise have trouble meeting, is much more in the nature of a good-will payment by the UK, which Dominic Raab MP, the erst-while lead government negotiator, says should only be paid if a satisfactory trade deal is agreed. The problem is then one of timing. The EU may well say that the only basis on which talks extend beyond March 2019 is if the UK agrees to pay the £39 billion in full – in addition to reaffirming its agreement to honour the commitments given by the UK government on the Irish border. A way round the money problem may be for the UK to commit to paying the roughly £20 billion which the government accepts is payable with the reminder only payable if a satisfactory deal is concluded but whether the EU would agree to this is far from certain. This is a rock on which the Brexit negotiations may yet founder.

If there is no majority in Parliament for any way ahead there may well be increased calls for a second referendum. There are already some key Labour figures, especially Chuka Umunna MP, who have strongly advoked this course of action and there were largely unsuccessful efforts at the September 2018 Labour Party Conference to make this official Labour Party policy. Whether this would be a wise move, however, is open to serious doubt because there are several very substantial problems about holding a second referendum. This is not a popular policy with the electorate and there are strong democratic grounds for saying that the 2016 referendum was decisive and that there should not be a repeat. There are also major practical problems. One is on timing. If the referendum is held after 29 March 2018, and by this time we are out of the EU, any proposal for us continuing membership would involve us reapplying to join rather than remaining in, reopening key questions about our rebate, a possible obligation to join the Euro and migration policy. There is also a major issue about what the choices on offer should be. Being in the EU or accepting the government's form of Brexit, but excluding a Canada type deal would outrage a very substantial proportion of the electorate, but having a three-way choice is clearly problematic, although not necessarily completely insoluble. The government stance is resolutely opposed to a second referendum. Although those favouring one being held appear to be confident that the result would be in favour of the UK continuing its membership of the EU, it is far from certain that this would in fact be the outcome.

So where does this leave Labour policy on Brexit? The party is clearly in considerable difficulty, torn in several different directions. Most MPs and party members would like to see the UK remaining in the Single Market and the Customs Union but the price of doing so may be very high in electoral terms. The reaction generally to the Chequers proposals, which looks like being the only practical way to this outcome, has been very negative not least in opinion polls suggesting what the voting consequences might be in future elections. While many Labour activists might like to see a second referendum being held, and won by the Remain side, tying the party to this policy looks risky and unpopular. However, voting against the government's Brexit proposals, if this leads to Parliament having no agreement on how to proceed, runs the serious risk of making the party look irresponsible and unpatriotic. Labour is, as the saying goes, between a rock and a hard place.

There are longer-term issues at stake here too. To what extent do the 37% of 2015 general election Labour voters who voted for Leave in 2016 regard our relationship with the EU as being of real importance? The 2016 referendum outcome, with its very high vote and the support which materialised among many people who had otherwise dropped out of taking part in elections, suggests that, for quite a lot of people, it may be more important than the Remain camp may suppose. Labour clearly has a big problem holding onto its traditional working-class base as the party membership becomes more metropolitan, highly educated, internationalist and middle class. Seeming to renege on the EU referendum outcome may be the last straw which breaks key electoral ties to Labour.

Finally, there is an overarching problem which somehow needs to be factored into what policies Labour chooses to support over the coming months. Ever since the UK joined what was then the EEC in 1973, we have had an ambivalent attitude to our membership. Our history, our traditions, our legal system and our island status have all made us uneasy partners. The result has been divisions affecting both our major parties which, over the last decades since we joined, have been a divisive and major distraction from many other things which needed to be done. The UK very badly needs to come to some settled relationship with the EU, which is broadly acceptable to most people in the UK – and among the EU27 – and which is going to last. Unfortunately, it does not look as though any of the choices which Parliament is going to have to confront are likely to achieve this kind of a result. As a result, Euroscepticism and Europhilia, with all the tensions and disagreements which they engender, are likely to last. This means that Labour's policy towards Europe needs to embrace not only trying to find some kind of short-term solution to where we are now, but also to look ahead to how to hold the coalition of interests which makes up the Labour Party together in a very deeply divided country and to avoid Europe being a constant dividing factor. This is not going to be an easy challenge to overcome.

## NOTES

1. OECD website.

2. Website: www.cvce.eu.

3. Wikipedia entry on Ernest Bevin

4. Wikipedia entry on Clement Atlee.

5. Wikipedia entry on the Messina Conference.

6. Burrage (2016, p. 8).

7. Wikipedia entry on the Treaty of Rome.

8. *International Financial Statistics* (1989, pp. 164–165).

9. ukandeu.ac.uk website.

10. ukandeu.ac.uk website.

11. Entry on *The Independent* website on Hugh Gaitskell's speeches.

12. Personal recollections of the author.

13. Wikipedia entry on the EU European Community membership referendum 1975.

14. Personal recollections of the author.

15. Wikipedia entry on Jacques Delors.

16. Pinder (2001).

17. Shipman (2016).

18. Details are on the Electoral Commission website.

19. Lord Ashcroft (2016).

20. Lord Ashcroft (2016).

21. BBC report: EU Referendum: Almost all North East areas vote for Brexit.

22. *The impact of immigration on occupational wages* (2015).

23. Shipman (2016).

24. BBC website report on EU electioneering.

25. Wikipedia entry: United Kingdom European Union membership referendum, 2016.

26. Details are on the Electoral Commission website.

27. Kinnock and Jervis (2018).

28. Details are on the Electoral Commission website.

29. Wikipedia entry on Theresa May's Lancaster House speech.

30. Explanatory article in *The Times* dated 6 April 2018.

31. Entry on the I news website.

32. BBC contemporaneous news reports.

33. Guardian website entry on the Prime Minister's Florence speech.

## REFERENCES

Ashcroft, L. (2016). *Well you did ask*. London: Biteback.

Bank of England (2015). In S. Nickell & J. Saleheen (Eds.), *The impact of immigration on occupational wages*. London: Bank of England.

Burrage, M. (2016). *The Eurosceptic' s handbook*. London: Civitas.

International Monetary Fund (1989). *International financial statistics*. Washington, DC: IMF.

Kinnock, S., & Jervis, J. (Eds.). (2018). *Spirit of Britain, Purpose of labour*. London: Labour Future.

Pinder, J. (2001). *The European Union: A very short introduction*. Oxford: Oxford University Press.

Shipman, T. (2016). *All out war.* London: William Collins.

# 5

# EXPLAINING THE BREXIT VOTE: A SOCIOECONOMIC AND PSYCHOLOGICAL EXPLORATION OF THE REFERENDUM VOTE

*David Hearne, Rebecca Semmens-Wheeler and Kimberley M. Hill*

## INTRODUCTION

Since the referendum on membership of the European Union (EU) in June 2016, research continues on the socioeconomic and psychological factors affecting the UK's decision. Although the vote to leave the EU appeared to mark a seismic shift in the UK polity, the forces that drove it were visible beforehand. The most powerful predictor of the share of the Leave vote in an area was support for UKIP in European Parliament elections two years previously (Goodwin & Heath, 2016).

Whilst a number of sociopolitical hypotheses have been proposed to explain the result, they are typically not grounded in psychological theory. This is curious, as our desire is to understand *why* the vote unfolded as it did. Therefore, most of the theories we mention in this chapter are explicitly sociopsychological. For example, whilst identity is individual, we understand ourselves by our interactions with others and so identity is deeply social. This cross-disciplinary chapter contributes to the academic debate around the UK's decision to leave the EU by providing a bridge between social science research and that on the psychological processes behind Brexit. We posit this as a 'first pass' at the problem, rather than delivering any final answers, considering a range of psychological factors and how these might relate to economic and demographic variables. In the material that follows, we articulate a simple model of the vote and conduct basic econometric analysis.

## A SIMPLE ECONOMETRIC MODEL OF THE BREXIT VOTE

Polling data suggest several demographic factors have significant associations with the probability that a person voted for Brexit (Ashcroft, 2016). Education, social class, and ethnicity all have predictive power (Ashcroft, 2016) and are highly correlated with one another. We want to disentangle the impact of each of them after controlling for the others and therefore posit a simple statistical model of the Brexit vote at the Local Authority (LA) level where we can run multivariate analysis of this nature. Like other similar studies (e.g. Becker, Fetzer, & Novy, 2017; Goodwin & Heath, 2016) we make use of aggregate data regressing explanatory variables on the percentage of eligible votes cast that were in favour of leaving the EU using data from the Electoral Commission (2016).

Aggregate data in this case replaces polling data, which are expensive to collect and subject to non-response bias, recall error, sampling difficulties and several other issues. Ultimately, analysis based on aggregate data cannot show the determinants of the vote at an individual level. Our results are thus suggestive rather than absolute and we cannot use them to infer causality. Theoretically, the fact that the dependent variable is a proportion poses a problem. However, in practice there are no predicted results outside the interval and Ordinary Least Squares (OLS) provides a linear model that should be locally appropriate. More problematic are issues of model selection and errors-in-variables. Although we have up-to-date information on many variables, these are statistical samples subject to measurement error. Future work will undoubtedly want to consider using instrumental variables estimation in order to avoid bias.

Hence, model selection is key: there are a plethora of variables that might be included and an entirely atheoretical approach is unlikely to be justified. To be truly rigorous, inference (in the mould of classical statistics) should not be on data already seen, although in practice it is impossible to ignore the results of other researchers with the same data. Becker et al. (2017) apply a best subset selection procedure to an OLS regression to derive a statistically sound model, including a number of innovative variables not previously seen in the literature.

## DATA

Given the findings of Ashcroft (2016), we include demographic data on ethnicity, education, age and a proxy for social class. Competition for scarce resources, austerity, immigration and a lack of opportunities in declining regions and 'places that don't matter' (Rodríguez-Pose, 2018, p. 189) could have had an impact on the Brexit vote, so we included variables capturing these.

Data on ethnicity were taken from the Annual Population Survey (henceforth APS) (ONS, 2017a). Whilst this contains data on several ethnic groups and the proportion born abroad, they have large coefficients of variation, which are likely to lead to inconsistent results (due to the errors-in-variables problem). Worse, some LAs have no result at all. Therefore, we instead consider the change in the proportion of the population which is 'white British' in each LA. These data are much more robust but do not allow us to consider European and non-European ethnic groups separately.

We consider the proportion of residents in each LA who were white British and the change in this proportion over 10 years. The former functions as our measure of ethnicity, whilst the latter is a measure of immigration intensity. Data on education are available from the same data source. In order to ensure comparability across the UK education by National Vocational Qualification (NVQ) equivalent are considered, including variables on the proportion of the population with NVQ4+ (broadly speaking equivalent to a degree) and those with an NVQ2 (equivalent to 5 A*-C GCSEs) or below. The APS contains data on the proportion of the population in Standard Occupational Classification (SOC) categories 1–3, which includes managers, professionals, associates and technical staff.[1]

Age data come from the ONS's population estimates. We include the proportion of over 65s and the proportion of under 30s in each LA. Also included is a measure of austerity originally posited by Becker et al. (2017), specifically the total reduction in benefit spending per working adult in each LA as reported by the Financial Times (2013) and a measure of pressure on a local public service – namely the proportion of National Health Service (NHS) cancer patients treated within 62 days (sourced from Becker et al., 2017).

Median income for residents of each LA is taken from the Annual Survey on Hours and Earnings (ONS, 2017b).

We take an average of median pay by LA over the past three years to minimise the errors-in-variables problem. Given evidence on the 'left-behind', we use several variables likely to be linked to economic strength and resilience including the change in median pay over the past decade (we use a three-year average and compare it to the same three-year period a decade earlier) from ASHE and the unemployment rate by LA, which is sourced from the APS.

The share of the economy made up by the manufacturing sector in 1998 (ONS, 2017c) is also used as a proxy for economic decay. Given the precipitous decline in manufacturing employment over the past 20 years it is probable that areas with a larger manufacturing base have been hardest hit by deindustrialisation. We also included the Leave vote share in 1975 as a variable alongside regional dummies.

## RESULTS

| Coefficient | Estimate |
|---|---|
| (Intercept) | 54.71** |
| | (11.75) |
| % of population who are white British | 0.23** |
| | (0.05) |
| % growth in full-time salaries over the past decade | −0.03 |
| | (0.04) |
| Median full-time salaries (in £1,000) | 0.04 |
| | (0.13) |
| % increase in the proportion of the population who are not white British over the past decade | 0.58** |
| | (0.09) |
| % with NVQ4+ | −0.47** |

(*Continued*)

| Coefficient | Estimate |
| --- | --- |
| | (0.09) |
| % over 65 | 0.14 |
| | (0.10) |
| % under 30 | −0.34** |
| | (0.09) |
| % who voted Leave in 1975 | 0.19** |
| | (0.07) |
| East Midlands dummy | 1.28 |
| | (1.03) |
| London dummy | 1.76 |
| | (1.83) |
| North East dummy | 1.04 |
| | (1.89) |
| North West dummy | −1.15 |
| | (1.40) |
| Scotland dummy | −14.54** |
| | (1.61) |
| South East dummy | 1.54 |
| | (0.99) |
| South West dummy | −1.53 |
| | (1.16) |
| Wales dummy | −3.68* |
| | (1.59) |
| West Midlands dummy | 2.55* |
| | (1.12) |
| Yorkshire & Humberside dummy | 1.61 |
| | (1.28) |
| % in SOC groups 1–3 | −0.15* |
| | (0.06) |

(*Continued*)

| Coefficient | Estimate |
|---|---|
| Proportion of cancer patients treated within 62 days | −0.09* |
| | (0.04) |
| Share of manufacturing in 1998 | 6.34 |
| | (3.99) |
| Unemployment Rate | 0.21 |
| | (0.18) |
| % with NVQ2 or below | 0.05 |
| | (0.09) |
| Estimated per capita austerity by region (in £100) | 0.06 |
| | 0.41 |

*Note*: Residual standard error: 4.148 on 301 degrees of freedom

(52 observations missing) ** = significant at 1% * = significant at 5%

$R^2$: 0.858, Adjusted $R^2$: 0.8467

Heteroscedasticity-robust standard errors were used. After controlling for the other factors, LAs with a higher proportion of people in the white British ethnic group tended to vote Leave more heavily. Each additional percentage point was associated with a 0.23 percentage point increase in the Leave vote. The change in the proportion of white Britons over the past decade in an area is negatively associated with the Leave vote. Whilst this might initially seem counterintuitive, the first variable is a measure of the ethnic composition of an area whereas the second is a measure of the change in ethnic composition and is strongly associated with migration. *Ceteris paribus*, exposure to immigration significantly increases the Leave vote of an area.

The proportion of highly educated individuals (NVQ4+) is strongly negatively related to the Leave vote but lower education levels appear to have little effect. The difference between those with A-levels and those who left school at 16 is not significant. Although a high proportion of under-30s is associated with a stronger Remain vote, the proportion of over-65s in an LA is not statistically significant after controlling for other factors (e.g. the lower education levels of this group). The latter chimes with the results of Liberini, Oswald, Proto, and Redoano (2017) who use a completely different dataset and methodology, giving confidence in the finding. More generally, these results fit nicely with the findings of Fielding (2018), who argues that find the inhabitants of areas with a high density of universities hold social views that are significantly more liberal than inhabitants of other areas.

We find that a higher vote in favour of leaving in 1975 is associated with a higher vote in favour of leaving in 2016, suggesting a degree of regional consistency over time. Nevertheless, this effect is quite weak and there is considerable heterogeneity. Given the large majority in favour of remaining in 1975, it is probable that many individuals must have changed their minds in order to deliver the Brexit result of today.

Being in Scotland was associated with a near 15 percentage point drop in the Leave share. Intriguingly, after controlling for demographic factors regions in Wales also voted Leave less strongly than equivalent regions in England (by around 3.7 percentage points). The only English region that differed from the rest was the West Midlands (which voted Leave more strongly than might be expected from its demographics). The proportion of an LA's population in SOC groups 1–3 was associated with a lower Leave vote, suggesting that occupation was an important marker. Finally, the proportion of cancer patients treated within 62 days was significant at the 5% level, although the effect was quantitatively small. This is indicative that public service provision *could* have affected the vote, although more evidence is needed before concrete judgements can be made. We cannot reject the null hypothesis that the coefficients on the remainder of the variables are zero (either individually or jointly), although they mostly have the expected signs. Inability to reject the null does not necessarily mean that these effects do not exist.

If we use a best subset selection procedure minimising the Schwartz-Bayesian Information Criterion (BIC) then we arrive at the following model:

| Coefficient | Estimate |
|---|---|
| (Intercept) | 79.38** |
| | (5.25) |
| % of population who are white British | 0.18** |
| | (0.03) |
| % increase in the proportion of the population who are not white British over the past decade | 0.53** |
| | (0.07) |
| % with NVQ4+ | −0.52** |
| | (0.05) |
| % under 30 | −0.43** |
| | (0.06) |
| Scotland dummy | −12.8** |
| | (0.91) |
| West Midlands dummy | 2.61** |
| | (0.70) |
| % in SOC groups 1–3 | −0.18** |
| | (0.05) |
| Proportion of cancer patients treated within 62 days | −0.11* |
| | (0.04) |

*Note*: Residual standard error: 4.353 on 366 degrees of freedom (three observations missing) ** = significant at 1% * = significant at 5%
$R^2$: 0.827, Adjusted $R^2$: 0.823

Again, errors are robust and coefficient interpretation is as above. Parsimony is a strength and the results of a RESET test give no reason to believe that higher-order terms would be useful predictors. This is reassuring given the inherent non-linearity of many of our variables. Also reassuring is the fact that coefficients have the same sign and similar magnitude to those in the larger model.

There remain a number of troubling econometric issues that future work will undoubtedly want to concentrate on in order to refine our understanding further. Future work will undoubtedly want to make heavier use of ward-level data and, although all efforts have been made to minimise errors-in-variables, researchers may wish to consider using instruments to avoid this problem entirely. Given the non-linearity of the dependent variable, researchers are likely to wish to experiment with non-linear regression, although this is unlikely to overturn any of the results found by ourselves and other researchers. Future work will also want to try and ascertain the individual level coefficients associated with several of these variables (e.g. how much does being a graduate reduce the probability that one voted for Brexit). Finally, further attention needs to be paid to how to measure labour market insecurity and precariousness, as well as perhaps using additional datasets to enhance our understanding.

## FACTORS UNDERLYING OUR RESULTS

We now employ a social psychological approach to understand the quantitative results above. Having identified variables that help to predict how likely an area was to vote Leave, we seek to understand *why* groups with these particular demographic characteristics may have felt particularly compelled to vote Leave. Our approach is partly informed by our ongoing qualitative research into the Brexit result. We now begin to interpret the results by turning to the key role that social identity appears to have played in the result.

## SOCIAL IDENTITY AND GROUP POLARISATION

It is widely believed that immigration was a key factor driving the decision to leave the EU (Goodwin & Milazzo, 2017). Research suggests that a perceived threat from immigrant 'out-groups' was a predictive factor in voting to Leave (Van de Vyver, Leite, Abrams, & Palmer, 2018). This perceived threat from immigration could have been accentuated by increases in immigration levels in areas with strong Leave votes (Goodwin & Heath, 2016; Goodwin & Milazzo, 2017).

Most evidence suggests that immigration has only modest (usually positive) effects on the wages of natives (Dustmann, Frattini, & Preston, 2013; Ottaviano & Peri, 2012) and European migration in particular has had a positive impact on the UK's fiscal position (Dustmann & Frattini, 2014). As a result, concern over migration is difficult to explain from the perspective of pure economic self-interest,[2] so contemporary research has tended to focus on other factors (McLaren & Johnson, 2007), implying that broader issues such as identity are likely to be at play here.

Social identity theory (SIT) was developed to account for how and why individuals from disadvantaged minority groups often do not directly confront dominant societal majority groups, even if their group is disadvantaged (Hogg & Abrams, 1988; Tajfel, 1978). The theory may help explain why those who were less likely to identify as European are more likely to vote Leave (Van de Vyver et al., 2018). SIT, suggests that a portion of an individual's self-concept is derived from their perceived or actual membership of certain social groups, as well as their non-membership to other groups. An influx of incomers can threaten self-identity, causing anxiety and negative contact encounters.

Class is another marker of identity. Those who self-identify as working-class tend to have more authoritarian and less pro-immigrant opinions (NatCen Social Research, 2016). These views are also typically associated with pro-Brexit voting patterns. Class is a fascinating avenue to explore, because Brexit has ignited passions that are difficult to reconcile with an issue that is primarily technical in nature (those whose eyes glaze over at a discussion of models of trade have suddenly found that membership of a customs union is an issue of profound and totemic importance to them).

A person's social identity and perceived threat from out-groups can influence voting intentions and behaviours (Van de Vyver et al., 2018). Research suggests that identity (and particularly English identity) is a crucial motivating factor for voting Leave (Henderson et al., 2016). One's social identity is important to health and wellbeing (Jetten, Haslam, & Haslam, 2012), but the perceived threat from those who do not share our social identity, or out-group members, can lead to some strong views. For example, one participant in our qualitative work on attitudes towards Brexit said,

> *The Islamic group is a clear and present danger to western civilization and it needs to be banned. It will never be assimilated or integrated and its stated aim is to overwhelm and out breed the indigenous peoples of Europe. (Semmens-Wheeler & Hill, In prep.)*

There certainly seems to be a sense of threat,

> *I am happy for immigrants to come to Britain. However, they should come with respect for the people who live here and respect our culture.*

*They should not come and expect the country to become more like their native country, because we're our own country with our own culture and our own principles. Britain should stay British, but welcome immigrants to share our cultural values, otherwise what makes Britain a separate country from other places in the world? (Semmens-Wheeler & Hill, In prep.)*

Fear about sharing economic and social resources has the potential to create group polarisation. Some evidence finds that unfavourable economic conditions are typically linked to stronger anti-immigrant sentiment (Meuleman, 2011; Semyonov, Raijman, & Gorodzeisky, 2006). The deep recession of 2008 and tepid recovery appears to have seen a hardening in attitudes towards immigration, perhaps because threat leads to increased in-group identification at the cost of the out-group (Castano, Yzerbyt, Paladino, & Sacchi, 2002).

Another psychological theory that could explain this phenomenon is Intergroup Threat Theory (Stephan, Ybarra, & Morrison, 2009), which suggests that prejudice and negative attitudes towards out-groups (e.g. immigrants) can be explained by both realistic threats and symbolic threats. The former influence physical wellbeing and the economic and political power of the in-group. The latter come from cultural differences in values, morals, worldviews and negative stereotypes about the out-group (Stephan et al., 2009). Additionally, intergroup anxiety is experienced by the in-group when interacting with out-group members. This theory could be used to explain how EU immigrants are seen as a potentially harmful out-group by non-EU-migrant in-groups, through the perceived competition for limited resources (i.e. realistic threat).

This, in turn, could lead to hostility towards the out-group, which may have been expressed in a vote to leave the EU. It is also possible that people voted for the EU against their own economic interests because of a perceived symbolic threat that the values of their in-group could be at risk. Other factors, like socioeconomic status (SES), can be linked to threat perceptions. For example, those with lower SES are more reactive to threat (Kraus, Horberg, Goetz, & Keltner, 2011). It is likely this was a contributory factor to the high proportion of Leave voters amongst lower SES groups (Skinner & Gottfried, 2016), particularly given that research has alluded to a 'geography of discontent' (Los, McCann, Springford, & Thissen, 2017). If certain areas are experiencing discontent due to perceived deprivation, slowing productivity and limited investment then this could be combined with fears related to immigration leading some to hypothesise that these left-behind areas drove the vote (Rodríguez-Pose, 2018). Given the strong incentives to relocate that a lack of local opportunity creates, it is unsurprising that individuals who remain in such areas feel that EU membership has not benefitted them. Low political trust amplifies existing anti-immigration sentiments (Abrams & Travaglino, 2018). In this context, it is significant that trust in politicians in the UK is near all-time lows and has fallen since the financial crisis and recession (Freeguard, 2015).

## LOCUS OF CONTROL

Research has shown that individuals with lower SES tend to have lower sense of control (Kraus, Piff, & Keltner, 2009), feel politically excluded and experience having less control over sociopolitical issues. They also tend to focus on external uncontrollable forces that influence their lives. Those with an external locus of control tend to have more anti-immigrant attitudes, which are related to (but distinct from) racial prejudice (Harell, Srokora, & Iyengar, 2017). This could contribute to blaming the EU, politicians, immigration, etc., for their life circumstances, and a chance to change the status quo by voting to leave the EU.

Populist movements have capitalised on the predicament of the left behind, arguing that the cosmopolitan elite disregard the lower, 'left-behind' classes, allowing low-skilled immigration to increase competition for jobs and failing to help communities to recover from the effects of recession (Lee, Morris, & Kemeny, 2018). Understandably, then, the 'left-behind' in Britain feel that they have little power over events in their lives. Participants in our own research described feeling that the areas in which they lived received little to no investment from the government. One man in a small town in Lincolnshire said 'All the money goes to London … all their transport links. We don't see any of the money.' (De Ruyter, Hearne, Guy, Semmens-Wheeler, & Goodwin, 2018, Forthcoming; Semmens-Wheeler & Hill, In prep.)

External locus of control in low SES areas may combine with lack of 'openness', a psychological trait that encompasses curiosity and an openness to new and unconventional ideas (McCrae & Costa, 2004). This trait is regionally clustered (Garretsen, Stoker, Soudis, Martin, & Rentfrow, 2018) and low levels of openness (characterised by preference for familiarity, routine and being relatively closed to new experiences) are seen in low SES areas. Higher levels of agreeableness and openness have been found to predict a Remain vote, whereas other traits, such as neuroticism and extraversion have been found to promote Leave votes. Particular regions also appear to have a higher anti-immigrant sentiment (Czaika & Di Lillo, 2018). There appears to be significant spatial dependence – proximate regions exhibit similar attitudes towards immigrants. Within the UK, London, the South East, Scotland and Northern Ireland all exhibit slightly lower anti-immigrant attitudes towards those of different ethnicity.

This does appear to coincide with regions where the vote in favour of Brexit was the least strong, raising the possibility of common factors. Certainly, London, the South East and Scotland all have educational attainment levels higher than other regions in Great Britain. Research suggests that graduates tend to have increased agreeableness, particularly if they are from disadvantaged backgrounds (Kassenboehmer, Leung, & Schurer, 2018) and a higher level of education has been linked to a higher locus of control (Smith, 2003). This is interesting given the links between Higher Education and voting preferences.

## SUMMARY AND CONCLUSIONS

Several factors appear to have had an impact on the Brexit vote. Our findings mirror earlier research with some nuances. Education was a crucial factor, as was exposure to immigration. After controlling for other variables, areas with a large young population tended to have a higher 'remain' vote, although the same does not appear to be true amongst the old, reinforcing the findings of Liberini et al. (2017). LAs in Scotland had a much lower propensity to vote Leave than other areas but the West Midlands voted Leave particularly strongly, even after accounting for demographic factors. Social class also appears to have played a strong role.

A variety of sociopsychological factors played a significant role in driving this, with social identity, group polarisation and intergroup threat theory all apparently driving some of the antipathy towards high levels of immigration. Similarly, groups experiencing a low locus of control appear to have voted Leave more strongly with low political trust amplifying these trends. The upshot is that work on understanding both the socioeconomic environment and psychological processes underlying the populist votes of the early twenty-first century, of which Brexit is just one, is still in its infancy and future cross-disciplinary collaboration is essential if we are to develop a holistic understanding of them.

## NOTES

1. This is widely seen as an acceptable proxy for those in so-called 'middle class' jobs.

2. Although there is something of a consensus in the literature, this view is by no means universally held (e.g. Borjas, 2003). There is some evidence that immigration may have had a modestly deleterious effect on incomes in the bottom two deciles (Dustmann et al., 2013) but this struggles to explain why immigration was such a salient issue for a majority of voters – particularly those above retirement age.

## REFERENCES

Abrams, D., & Travaglino, G. A. (2018). Immigration, political trust, and Brexit – Testing an aversion amplification hypothesis. *British Journal of Social Psychology*, *57*(2), 310–326. doi:10.1111/bjso.12233

Antonucci, L., Horvath, L., Kutiyski, Y., & Krouwel, A. (2017). The malaise of the squeezed middle: Challenging the narrative of the 'left behind' Brexiter. *Competition and Change*, *21*(3), 211–229. doi:10.1177/1024529417704135

Ashcroft, M. (2016). *How the United Kingdom voted on Thursday … and why*. Retrieved from https://lordashcroftpolls. com/2016/06/how-the-united-kingdom-voted-and-why/

Becker, S. O., Fetzer, T., & Novy, D. (2017). Who voted for Brexit? A comprehensive district-level analysis. *Economic Policy*, *32*(92), 601–650. doi:10.1093/epolic/eix012

Borjas, G. J. (2003). The labor demand curve is downward sloping: Reexamining the impact of immigration on the labor market*. *The Quarterly Journal of Economics*, *118*(4), 1335–1374. doi:10.1162/003355303322552810

Castano, E., Yzerbyt, V., Paladino, M.-P., & Sacchi, S. (2002). I belong, therefore, I exist: Ingroup identification, ingroup entitativity, and ingroup bias. *Personality and Social Psychology Bulletin*, *28*(2), 135–143. doi:10.1177/0146167202282001

Czaika, M., & Di Lillo, A. (2018). The geography of anti-immigrant attitudes across Europe, 2002–2014. *Journal of Ethnic and Migration Studies*, *44*(15), 2453–2479. doi: 10.1080/1369183X.2018.1427564

De Ruyter, A., Hearne, D., Guy, J., Semmens-Wheeler, R., & Goodwin, B. (in prep.). *Tales from an episodic journey into 'Brexitland': Understanding the underlying factors as to why people voted 'Leave'*. CBS Working Paper, in prep.

Dustmann, C., & Frattini, T. (2014). The fiscal effects of immigration to the UK. *The Economic Journal*, *124*(580), F593–F643. doi:10.1111/ecoj.12181

Dustmann, C., Frattini, T., & Preston, I. P. (2013). The effect of immigration along the distribution of wages. *The Review of Economic Studies*, *80*(1), 145–173. doi:10.1093/restud/rds019

Electoral Commission. (2016). *EU referendum results*. Retrieved from https://www.electoralcommission.org.uk/

find-information-by-subject/elections-and-referendums/
past-elections-and-referendums/eu-referendum/
electorate-and-count-information

Fielding, D. (2018). 1066 and all that: Some deep
determinants of voting shares in the 2016 referendum on
EU membership. *The World Economy, 41*(4), 1131–1146.
doi:10.1111/twec.12621

Financial Times (Producer). (2013). *FT austerity audit.*
Retrieved from https://ig.ft.com/austerity-map/

Freeguard, G. (2015, 5 February). *Public trust in
public servants – in six graphs*. Retrieved from
https://www.instituteforgovernment.org.uk/blog/
public-trust-public-servants-%E2%80%93-six-graphs

Garretsen, H., Stoker, J. I., Soudis, D., Martin, R. L., &
Rentfrow, P. J. (2018). Brexit and the relevance of regional
personality traits: More psychological openness could have
swung the regional vote. *Cambridge Journal of Regions,
Economy and Society, 11*(1), 165–175. doi:10.1093/cjres/rsx031

Goodwin, M., & Heath, O. (2016). The 2016 Referendum,
Brexit and the left behind: An aggregate-level analysis
of the result. *The Political Quarterly, 87*(3), 323–332.
doi:10.1111/1467-923X.12285

Goodwin, M., & Milazzo, C. (2017). Taking back control?
Investigating the role of immigration in the 2016 vote for
Brexit. *The British Journal of Politics and International
Relations, 19*(3), 450–464. doi:10.1177/1369148117710799

Greenberg, J., Pyszczynski, T., & Solomon, S. (1986). The
causes and consequences of a need for self-esteem: A terror
management theory. In R. F. Baumeister (Ed.), *Public self and
private self* (pp. 189–212). New York, NY: Springer-Verlag.

Harell, A., Srokora, S., & Iyengar, S. (2017). Locus of control and anti-immigrant sentiment in Canada, the United States, and the United Kingdom. *Political Psychology*, *38*(2), 345–360.

Henderson, A., Jeffery, C., Liñeira, R., Scully, R., Wincott, D., & Wyn Jones, R. (2016). England, Englishness and Brexit. *The Political Quarterly*, *87*(2), 187–199. doi:10.1111/1467-923X.12262

Hogg, M. A., & Abrams, D. (1988). *Social identifications: A social psychology of intergroup relations and group processes*. London: Routledge.

Jetten, J., Haslam, C., & Haslam, S. A. (2012). *The social cure: Identity, health and well-being*. Hove: Psychology Press.

Kassenboehmer, S. C., Leung, F., & Schurer, S. (2018). University education and non-cognitive skill development. *Oxford Economic Papers*, *70*(2), 538–562. doi:10.1093/oep/gpy002

Kraus, M. W., Horberg, E. J., Goetz, J. L., & Keltner, D. (2011). Social class rank, threat vigilance, and hostile reactivity. *Personality and Social Psychology Bulletin*, *37*(10), 1376–1388. doi:10.1177/0146167211410987

Kraus, M. W., Piff, P. K., & Keltner, D. (2009). Social class, sense of control, and social explanation. *Journal of Personality and Social Psychology*, *97*(6), 992–1004. doi:10.1037/a0016357

Lee, N., Morris, K., & Kemeny, T. (2018). Immobility and the Brexit vote. *Cambridge Journal of Regions, Economy and Society*, *11*(1), 143–163. doi:10.1093/cjres/rsx027

Liberini, F., Oswald, A., Proto, E., & Redoano, M. (2017). *Was Brexit caused by the unhappy and the old?* CAGE Working Paper 342, Warwick University.

Los, B., McCann, P., Springford, J., & Thissen, M. (2017). The mismatch between local voting and the local economic consequences of Brexit. *Regional Studies*, 51(5), 786–799. doi:10.1080/00343404.2017.1287350

McCrae, R. R., & Costa, P. T. (2004). A contemplated revision of the NEO five-factor inventory. *Personality and Individual Differences*, 36(3), 587–596. doi:https://doi.org/10.1016/S0191-8869(03)00118-1

McLaren, L., & Johnson, M. (2007). Resources, group conflict and symbols: Explaining anti-immigration hostility in Britain. *Political Studies*, 55(4), 709–732. doi:10.1111/j.1467-9248.2007.00680.x

Meuleman, B. (2011). Perceived economic threat and anti-immigration attitudes: Effects of immigrant group size and economic conditions revisited. In E. Davidov, P. Schmidt, & J. Billiet (Eds.), *Cross cultural analysis: Methods and applications*. New York, NY: Routledge.

Milliard, R. (2014). Are you stuck in the squeezed middle? Why we're feeling the pinch like never before. *Daily Mail*. Retrieved from https://www.dailymail.co.uk/home/you/article-2575538/Are-stuck-Squeezed-Middle-Why-feeling-pinch-like-never-before.html

NatCen Social Research. (2016). *British social attitudes. 33*. Retrieved from http://www.bsa.natcen.ac.uk/latest-report/british-social-attitudes-33/introduction.aspx

Office for National Statistics. (2017a). *Annual population survey Jan–Dec 2016*. Retrieved from https://www.nomisweb.co.uk/query/construct/summary.asp?mode=construct&version=0&dataset=17. Accessed on August 22, 2018.

Office for National Statistics. (2017b). *Annual survey of hours and earnings: Table 8, 1997–2016*. Retrieved from

https://www.ons.gov.uk/employmentandlabourmarket/
peopleinwork/earningsandworkinghours/datasets/
placeofresidencebylocalauthorityashetable8

Office for National Statistics. (2017c). *Regional gross value
added (balanced), UK: 1998 to 2016*. Retrieved from https://
www.ons.gov.uk/economy/grossvalueaddedgva/bulletins/regi
onalgrossvalueaddedbalanceduk/1998to2016

Ottaviano, G. I. P., & Peri, G. (2012). Rethinking the effect
of immigration on wages. *Journal of the European
Economic Association, 10*(1), 152–197. doi:10.1111/j.
1542-4774.2011.01052.x

Rodríguez-Pose, A. (2018). Commentary: The revenge of
the places that don't matter (and what to do about it).
*Cambridge Journal of Regions, Economy and Society,
11*(1),189–209. doi:10.1093/cjres/rsx024

Semmens-Wheeler, R., & Hill, K. (In prep.). *Understanding
the perceptions of voters in rural and regional England on
Brexit*.

Semyonov, M., Raijman, R., & Gorodzeisky, A. (2006).
The rise of anti-foreigner sentiment in European Societies,
1988–2000. *American Sociological Review, 71*(3), 426–449.
doi:10.1177/000312240607100304

Skinner, G., & Gottfried, G. (2016). *How Britain
voted in the 2016 EU referendum*. Retrieved
from https://www.ipsos.com/ipsos-mori/en-uk/
how-britain-voted-2016-eu-referendum

Smith, V. L. (2003). *Analysis of locus of control and
educational level utilizing the internal control index*. Theses,
Dissertations and Capstones, Paper 881.

Stephan, W. G., Ybarra, O., & Morrison, K. R. (2009). Intergroup threat theory. In T. D. Nelson (Ed.), *Handbook of prejudice, stereotyping, and discrimination*. Hove: Taylor & Francis.

Strauss, D. (2018). Squeezed middle faces growing risk of poverty: OECD research shows widening divide between the lower and upper middle classes. *Financial Times*. Retrieved from https://www.ft.com/content/13fe209e-707f-11e8-852d-d8b934ff5ffa

Tajfel, H. (1978). *Differentiation between social groups: Studies in the social psychology of intergroup relations*. London: Academic Press [for] European Association of Experimental Social Psychology.

Van de Vyver, J., Leite, A. C., Abrams, D., & Palmer, S. B. (2018). Brexit or Bremain? A person and social analysis of voting decisions in the EU referendum. *Journal of Community & Applied Social Psychology*, 28(2), 65–79. doi:10.1002/casp.2341

# 6

# CUSTOM UNIONS AND COMMON MARKETS AS ECONOMIC SECURITY FAULT LINES. THE GARLIC CASE

*Stefania Paladini*

One of the most heated discussions regarding Brexit points at the future of the trade deal that UK is going to sign with the EU. There have been endless discussions since the day of the referendum results in June 2016 about this crucial aspect, and nothing has been so far agreed. Some analysts, however, have already pointed out to a series of issues that any change in the structure of the EU market can cause.

The case analysed in the following pages wants to serve as a cautionary tale, and there is an important reason for that: it is a good illustration of all kinds of issues that can happen when countries are members of some kind of regional associations but not of others and whose consequences can produce spillovers from pure trade matters to more serious security concerns.

It is not very often that something as common as the import–export of agricultural products – such as non-exotic fruits and vegetables – becomes the object of such a dispute across multiple states. This is what happened in the now infamous case of the Chinese garlic export, which has seen in the last 20 years, several instances of smuggling, conviction, and frauds all over Europe, even though most incidents have taken place mainly in the North Sweden, Norway, the UK and Ireland. There is a reason for that, which will be explained below.

## 1. GARLIC. A CONTROVERSIAL CROP

Common or not, garlic is an important commodity.

The estimates of world production in 2017 were of about 23 million tons (Eurostat, 2018), 80% of them produced by China. A quick look at the statistics show that the production has grown impressively over the last 20 years, even though not with a linear progression.

The second world producer, India, produced about 1.25 million tonnes, followed by South Korea, the United States (with production mostly concentrated in California), Egypt and the Russian Federation. While these and several other countries produce a certain quantity of garlic for internal consumption, not all of them manage to export it. This explains why, having a look at the world top exporters, the countries in the ranking are not the same of the ones above.

In 2017, global exports of garlic amounted at US$3.1 billion in 2017, up by 52% for all garlic shippers over the five-year period starting in 2013, even though 2017 has seen an overall decline both in quantity and prices.

China is the only country that appears in both lists.

The world market has been increasingly concentrated and in these last years about 75–80% of the garlic sold around the world has been exported from China (FaoStat, 2017). Parallel to this concentration, and somehow related to that, during the last 10 years the price of garlic has been constantly rising, due to a series of factors, first of all of declining world production and relative scarcity of supply.

Garlic prices in and outside China are very volatile and they account for the oscillatory production and exports curves over the reporting period, as shown in Fig. 1.[1]

More recently, due to minor crops in 2015 in China's region of Shandong and Jinxiang (the main producers), market prices spiralled in 2016 and 2017 in China and they were reflected in the spike in value in 2016 exports (FreshPlaza, 2017).

Together with China, a few European countries to figures prominently in the 2017 world top exporter list, and namely Spain (US$355.2 million, about 11.3% of the world export), Netherlands (US$96.1 million, 3.1%), France (US$41 million, 1.3%) and Italy (US$33.5 million, 1.1%). In addition to them, South America also manages to export large quantities,

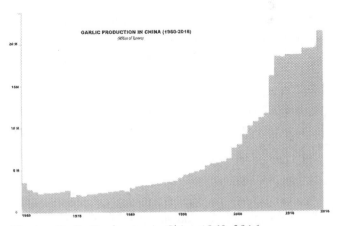

Fig. 1.   Garlic Production in China 1960–2016.
*Source*: Author elaboration on FAO data.

especially Argentina (US$182.8 million, 5.8%), and Chile, Mexico and Peru. In 2017, United States only contributed US$20.3 million (0.6%) to the world market.

Looking more in detail at Europe, Table 1 shows the statistics of the total production and import of garlic in the EU, both in value and quantity, to account for the fluctuations in the exchange rate over a period of 18 years. As a whole, the (EU) countries produce around 300,000 tonnes, approximately one-third of which comes from Spain, followed by Italy and France.

According to UN-Comtrade statistics,[2] in 2017 the garlic import in Europe fell 13.01% in comparison to 2016 (in quantity; in current US$, the decline was more marked, of about 17.9%), with imports that decreased to 47,880,356 kg. This result came in a counter-trend compared to the past, since a look at the time-series shows that the imports have increased 6.57% during the last 18 years. That growth was more marked in the first years of the century, with a record of 99,344,720 kg in 2003. That peak has never been reached afterwards. Successive decline has taken the level of the imports to almost the same amount of year 2000, where they were down at 44,92,704 million kg (Figs. 2 and 3).

On the other end, in 2017 exports have gone up 8.85%, from 67,428,432 kg to 73,393,896 kg, reaching an 18-year peak (the whole period saw an overall growth of 109.31%, with a minimum point of 6,073,421 kg in 2006).

But the statistics do not return the full picture; administrative procedures – mainly import licences and certificates of origin – and custom duties have a long and complicated story starting in the early 1990s.

The endgame is that, at present, the garlic sector in the EU is subjected to complex regulations, where both central bureaucracy and customs are involved in its implementation, and which previews both financial and administrative obligations

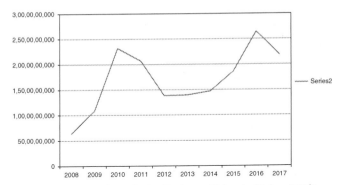

Fig. 2.   Export of Fresh Garlic from China in Value (US$).
*Source*: Author elaboration on EU COMTRADE data.

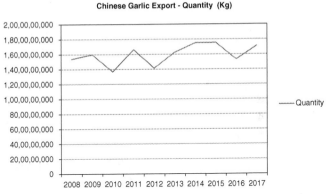

Fig. 3.   Export of Fresh Garlic from China in Quantity (kg).
*Source*: Author elaboration on EU COMTRADE data

to fulfil. In addition to that, there are heavy duties involved
for some garlic products, making the whole trading operation
often challenging to handle for exporters. This has fuelled a
series of illegal exports and smuggling that takes advantages
of the fact that some destination countries in Europe are not
also part of the EU Customs Union, therefore using the duty
differential among them to make a profit.

Table 1.   Tariff quotas opened pursuant to Decisions 2001/404/EC, 2006/398/EC, 2014/116/EU and (EU) 2016/243 for imports of garlic falling within CN code 0703 20 00

| Origin | Order number | Quota (tonnes) | | | | |
|---|---|---|---|---|---|---|
| | | First subperiod (June to August) | Second subperiod (September to November) | Third subperiod (December to February) | Fourth subperiod (March to May) | Total |
| **Argentina** | | | | | | **19 147** |
| Traditional importers | 09.4104 | — | — | 9 590 | 3 813 | |
| New importers | 09.4099 | — | — | 4110 | 1 634 | |
| *Total* | | — | — | *13 700* | *5 447* | |
| **China** | | | | | | **48 225** |
| Traditional importers | 09.4105 | 8 664 | 8 664 | 7 548 | 8 884 | |
| New importers | 09.4100 | 3 713 | 3 713 | 3 233 | 3 806 | |
| *Total* | | *12 377* | *12377* | *10 781* | *12 690* | |
| **Other third countries** | | | | | | **6 023** |
| Traditional importers | 09.4106 | 941 | 1 960 | 929 | 386 | |
| New importers | 09.4102 | 403 | 840 | 398 | 166 | |
| *Total* | | *1 344* | *2 800* | *1 327* | *552* | |
| **Total** | | **13 721** | **15 177** | **25 808** | **18 689** | **73 395** ’ |

The story starts back in the 1990s, when, in order to protect the EU internal market, the EU customs imposes a duty
on foreign garlic. There was a sound reason for that: the duty-
free entry of Chinese garlic into the EU nearly destroyed the
domestic garlic sector at that moment.

In 1993, the EU Commission, after requests from European
garlic producers – mainly Spain – and in order to avoid domestic garlic producers in EU member countries being displaced in
their home markets by a flood of cheap Chinese garlic products
(up to three times cheaper than the Spanish garlic), started to
establish a system of custom barriers, that evolved over time and
that works in a complicated way. The system was further geared
up in 2001 when China entered the World Trade Organisation
(WTO), with tariffs and duties that made Chinese garlic very
expensive for importers.

There is now a variety of import duty rates on garlic
products in the range of 10–15% of the Cost, Insurance, and
Freight (CIF) value, distributed through the various Combined Nomenclature (CN) codes as specified below.

There is a 9.6% duty on fresh or chilled garlic (CN code
0703 20 00), to which importers need to add an extra levy
of €1,200 per tonne, even though this additional tax is only
applicable to imports that exceed the annual quota of 73,395
tonnes worldwide (and of 48,225 tonnes in the case of China;
EU, 2016).[3]

Other kind of garlic products (CN code ex 0703 90 00
and following) does attract different treatments and namely:
14.4% on frozen garlic; 9.6% on preserved garlic; and, finally,
12.8% on dried garlic.

The rationale behind all these taxes, especially the 1,200
levy, was, by far now the most important threat – even though
not only one – to them. There are also quotas allocated to
other producers, such Argentinian garlic, the country where
most of the non-Chinese garlic comes from to the EU. Garlic

from Argentina is more expensive than the Chinese variety and it is produced in a minor quantity. Finally, there are countries that benefit from preferential agreements with the EU, such as Morocco, and that can export garlic in duty-free regime to the EU, although in small quantities.

The system is complicated by the fact that, in order to use quotas, Chinese exporters need to apply for an authorisation to the EU customs, which distribute the quotas among the applicants while, for exports that exceed the quota, it is necessary to apply in advance for the so-called B, license, and paying the fee of €1,200 per tonne.

Issues and frauds regarding garlic imports in the EU are nothing new, but, if the European Anti-Fraud Office (OLAF), the authority in charge of dealing with garlic irregularities, is to be trusted, while problems with Chinese garlic have started since the 1990s, but the imposition of the above-mentioned €1,200 levy in 2001 have made things substantially worse in terms of smuggling.

According to OLAF's estimates in 2006, at least €60 million had been already lost from Chinese garlic smuggling, and since then the case of smuggling have proliferated.

> *At the time of the estimate, among all agriculture-related investigations by the European Anti-fraud Office, Chinese garlic ranked third in number of cases, just behind sugar and meat. (GRO, 2016, online)*

It is likely that at present the whole garlic fraud has surpassed them.[4]


## 2. THE SMUGGLING RINGS

Also interesting is how the garlic has been smuggled from China to the EU in the last two decades, which has in a way followed the evolution of the barrier systems and changed over the years.

The traditional and most common way is the co-called 'origin fraud', where exporters lie about the origin of the garlic itself, declaring it as coming from countries other than China, generally one of those that benefit from treaties of association with the EU and to which no duties are levied.

That would be the case of garlic from Turkey, Egypt and Morocco – countries that have some sort of preferential, no-tariff agreements with the EU and which already produce garlic themselves – and from some Central and the South-American countries mentioned above – Peru, Chile, Mexico and Argentina. In all these cases, the Chinese garlic is first exported there and then reloaded into new containers before arriving in the EU.

But instances have been recorded also with Norway and Thailand, countries from which the EU has never imported garlic, and it is actually these cases that have raised the suspicion of the EU and led to the convictions.

There are other ways of smuggling, though.

One consists in 'misdeclaring' the product – for example, making fresh garlic pass as something else – such as apples, onions, ginger or even other, less-taxed variety of garlic products, such as frozen or dried garlic.[5]

Finally, there have been many instances, especially in the last 10 years, of full-fledged smuggling, where no declaration whatsoever has been filed and that have reached the general attention with some large-scale police operations. According to some estimates, about 100 tonnes of garlic have illegally transited through the EU border, avoiding several million in taxes before a smuggler was first caught in 2010. On that occasion, the smuggler carried 28 tonnes of Chinese garlic – for value of 500,000 Swedish crowns (about US$68,000) in unpaid import duties – over the Svinesundsbron Bridge that connects Sweden and Norway (Sveriges Radio, 2010).

Since then, arrests have increased.

In a famous instance, Paul Begley, one of the Ireland's top food producers, was arrested in 2011 and sentenced to six years in March 2012 (BBC News, 2012a) for saving €1.6 million in garlic taxes between September 2003 and October 2007. The fraud was discovered when a customs officer in Dublin examined a container from China allegedly declaring apples but containing fresh garlic.

That one was not a unique occurrence. There have been more recent cases of smuggling since then. Again in 2012, this time in December two men in London were convicted to six-year jail term due to €2.5 million (£2 million) of unpaid import duty (BBC News, 2012b). Instead of declaring garlic, they wrote on the import declaration that the goods were instead 'fresh ginger', which on the other hand, is a vegetable that attracts zero import duty.

Finally, supplies were shipped from China to Norway in 2013 – a non-EU state, where no garlic import taxes are applied – and then smuggled into neighbouring Sweden and the rest of the EU by lorry, thus avoiding EU import duties (BBC News, 2013). The Swedish police estimated that the two men – British nationals – managed to avoid €10 million in Swedish taxes through the scheme.

As recently as May 2018, the Thai military has been caught smuggling garlic to the country from China and other neighbouring countries (Sky News, 2018). While it is unclear which was the final destination of the smuggled garlic, it is not unlikely to imagine some of the goods may have ended up in the EU, as in the past.

In order to address this conundrum, which seems unlikely to find a solution by itself, the EU Commission has since 2016 been working on a plan to simplify the regime for the import of garlic in Europe. The idea would be to remove the harsh €1,200 levy that has proved to be more harmful than beneficial, let alone effective to curb imports, and therefore the need to apply for the license.

There are people who observe that, while important, Chinese garlic and the garlic produced and sold in the EU are not direct competitors. For a start, the majority of Chinese exports are unprocessed (fresh or chilled garlic), not other products. Moreover, 'green', non-tariff barriers seem to work well to restrict imports, especially when they come as international quality standards enforceable by inspection and searching for pesticide residue in the garlic.

Countries have been asking for a series of tests, among them the EU, whose 124 tests represent a measure even higher than Japan (Produce Reports, 2018).

In this way, the imports themselves would become purely a customs matter without a complex and time-consuming administrative procedure. Not everybody agrees on this need for simplification: a few garlic producers from the member states in the South of the EU have protested against the proposal, especially the ones from Spain.

The garlic case does not look close to a solution, and the smuggling incidents are likely to continue in the foreseeable future.

## 3. BEYOND GARLIC: THE WAY FORWARD

As mentioned at the beginning, it is difficult to tell at this stage what kind of asset a post-Brexit Europe will have between the EU and the UK. What is certain is that border issues will become paramount and could potentially be very challenging to handle, as the case of garlic illustrates more than well. It is not by chance that Norway, a non-EU country part of the Common Market, but NOT of the Customs Union, is the access point and together the key to the smuggling ring.

A non-EU UK which still remains part of the Common Market will of course open itself to similar kind of cases, notably over the border between Ireland and Northern Ireland, and, to a minor degree, at the ports of Felixstowe, Dover and Holyhead, where, barring some technological innovation that will allow for automatic goods control, things are going to become unpractical quite soon.

Possible solutions in this sense, of the kind already existing at the border between Sweden and Norway, are IT systems that declare goods before they even leave the warehouse in the country of origin, communications networks such as the Scandinavian Nordnet used by the 1,300 customs officials to joint-check the border, and anti-smuggling, x-ray scanners for lorries inspection (BBC News, 2017).

But things can still prove tricky, simply because the volume of trade is of a different scale between the UK and the rest of EU, and even technology solutions might prove insufficient.

The main issue here is that, once out of the EU, the UK will have the faculty to lower its tariffs over a series of non-sensitive goods, garlic being one of the many (same as Norway, the UK does not produce a great deal of it; Lexology, 2018). In any instance where tariffs are lower, smuggling can become an issue.

The fact of having a good relationship between the two custom enforcement agencies will not make a great deal of difference in this sense, as the case of Norway and Sweden (whose cooperation over a thousand-mile frontier, the EU's longest land border is exemplary[6]) does show.

Another possibility is some sort of customs union between the EU and the UK.

While it is somehow taken for granted that a non-EU country cannot be in the EU Customs Union (CU) – neither Norway nor Switzerland are, as a matter of fact – there are precedents here, as in the case of Turkey. Turkey, which has now an associate status with the EU and has applied for membership (but not granted so far, and not in the immediate future) enjoys a partial customs union that covers the majority of manufacturing goods and some, but not all, food products (and not agricultural and fisheries for example).

> *The implementation of the customs union (CU) in 1995 marked a key moment in the trade relationship between the EU and Turkey. The CU with Turkey was the EU's first substantial functioning CU with a non-member state and was one of the earliest attempts by the EU to share some of its legal system with another country. Turkey is also one of just three countries that have entered into a CU with the EU prior to becoming a candidate country. Under the CU, Turkey adopted the EU's common external tariff (CET) for most industrial products, as well as for the industrial components of agricultural products, and both the EU and Turkey agreed to eliminate all customs duties, quantitative restrictions and charges with equivalent effect on their bilateral trade. (World Bank, 2014, p. 23)*

The above-mentioned World Bank report also highlighted other important points, first of all the fact that the custom union accounted for more beneficial results for both countries than a free trade agreement.

The UK could seek a similar agreement, which could include, or not, an inclusion in the Common Market as in the case of Norway. Businesses that rely on complex and regional-based supply chains, such as car manufacturing, pharmaceutical sector and aerospace, just to mention the most important ones from the UK point of view, would certainly benefit from a custom union agreement. There are, of course, some drawbacks.

> *Turkey is still bound by the trade agreements the*
> *EU does around the world, and when new EU deals*
> *open up the Turkish market to companies from other*
> *countries, Turkey doesn't automatically get reciprocal*
> *rights for its companies. There are still long delays*
> *at Turkey's land border with the EU as well, because*
> *Turkey is not in the single market. Labour argues*
> *that the UK is a much bigger economy that could*
> *get a much better deal than Turkey, but there's no*
> *sign that the EU would allow the UK to continue to*
> *negotiate all its own trade agreements if such a deal*
> *was to be done. (BBC News, 2018, online)*

As of 4 October 2018, the day this chapter has been completed, a whole UK territory remaining inside the EU customs union – and not only Northern Ireland, as in some earlier proposal – seems to be more than just another possibility, and it has already elicited some substantial backing (City Am, 2018).

The measure is intended to be as temporary, while a full-fledged ad hoc treaty is negotiated between the EU and the UK. Other considerations apart, this latter solution would probably have the positive effect of avoiding some blatant cases of smuggling like the garlic case, together with addressing in a less controversial way the complex UK–Ireland border situation.

## NOTES

1. It is however the case to notice that, while year-on-year production figures vary a great deal due to the single harvests, the overall amount of garlic produced in China has risen by three times from 1970 to 2013, leading to the present market concentration.

2. EUROSTAT, the EU statistics office, gives different figures as it calculates them differently and only for the 28 EU countries. However, the two are comparable. For EUROSTAT's garlic data, see: https://ec.europa.eu/eurostat/data/database. Other statistics were taken from EU Comtrade and https://www.worldatlas.com.

3. The original quotas were substantially lower (EU Regulation 2014/2243) but they were adjusted in December 2016. Even that did not curb the demand for Chinese garlic and the smuggling that surfaced as a result.

4. To be sure, it is not just the EU that had huge problems with garlic import. Other countries, such as the US and South Korea, battled China's less-expensive goods with heavy tariffs. The US slapped a 377% tariff in the 1990s, opening the country to a flood of smuggling and damaging the local industry in California. In 2014,

> *a single Chinese company has flooded the U.S. market with 60 million pounds of garlic, almost half of it through the Port of Oakland, in a scheme to avoid penalties that protect domestic growers. (SFGate, 2014, online)*

> *South Korea followed in 1999 with 315% of tariffs (WSJ, 2000) before signing an agreement with China in the 2000s.*

5. One of these cases involved the UK directly.

> *The UK, for example, was fined 15 million pounds by the EU for failing to charge enough duty on Chinese garlic imports. These imports were classified as frozen garlic, which has a lower tariff rate than fresh garlic. Custom duties are collected by EU member states on behalf of the EU and paid to the common EU budget as part of each member state's annual contributions. As Brexit will allow the UK to negotiate its own trade deals with non-EU countries, it will be interesting to see how the country chooses*

*to manage its garlic trade. (GRO, 2016, online)*

6. According to some data, the average waiting time at the popular crossing point at Svinesund is about eight minutes (BBC, 2017).

## REFERENCES

BBC News. (2012a). Ireland garlic scam: Paul Begley jailed for six years. *BBC News*, March 10. Retrieved from https://www.bbc.co.uk/news/world-europe-17320460. Accessed on March 14, 2018.

BBC News. (2012b). Garlic smuggler flees conviction for £2m ginger fraud. *BBC News,* December 10. Retrieved from https://www.bbc.co.uk/news/business-20667816. Accessed on March 14, 2018.

BBC News. (2013). Who, what, why: Why do criminals smuggle garlic? *BBC News,* January 12. Retrieved from https://www.bbc.co.uk/news/magazine-20976887. Accessed on March 14, 2018.

BBC News. (2017). Frictionless borders: Learning from Norway. *BBC News*, September 29. Retrieved from https://www.bbc.com/news/av/technology-41413291/frictionless-borders-learning-from-norway. Accessed on October 01, 2018.

BBC News. (2018). Brexit: Why is the customs union so important?, *BBC News*, April 26. Retrieved from https://www.bbc.co.uk/news/uk-43871319. Accessed on October 01, 2018.

CityAM. (2018). Plan to keep all of UK in EU customs union after Brexit welcomed by Dublin in Irish backstop row. *CityAM,* October 4. Retrieved from http://www.cityam.com/264649/plan-keep-all-uk-eu-customs-union-after-brexit-welcomed. Accessed on October 04, 2018.

EUROSTAT. (2018). Online EU statistics database. Retrieved from https://ec.europa.eu/eurostat. Accessed on October 01, 2018.

EU. (2016). *Commission Implementing Regulation 2016/2243 of 13 December 2016 amending Regulation (EC) No. 341/2007 as regards the import tariff quota for garlic originating in China* (14 December 2016). Retrieved from https://eur-lex.europa.eu/eli/reg_impl/2016/2243/oj. Accessed on March 14, 2018.

EU. (2017). European Commission TARIC measure information (28 April 2017). Retrieved from https://ec.europa.eu/taxation_customs/business/calculation-customs-duties/what-is-common-customs-tariff/taric_en. Accessed on March 14, 2018.

FAO. (2017). *FAOSTAT* Crop. Retrieved from http://www.fao.org/faostat/en/#data/QC. Accessed on October 01, 2018.

Fresh Plaza. (2017). *China: Garlic export prices slide*. Retrieved from http://www.freshplaza.com/article/172051/China-Garlic-export-prices-slide. Accessed on October 01, 2018.

GRO. (2016). *The EU reeks of contraband garlic*, 15 July 2016. Retrieved from https://www.gro-intelligence.com/insights/the-eu-reeks-of-contraband-garlic. Accessed on March 14, 2018.

Lexology. (2017). *The UK's customs proposals: Do they pass the garlic smuggling test? – Lexology*. Retrieved from https://www.lexology.com/library/detail.aspx?g=5a5a8399-c60f-443c-9b93-c3e5b11ab1bb. Accessed on March 14, 2018.

Produce Reports. (2018). 2017 year in review: China's fresh garlic. Retrieved from export.https://www.producereport.com/article/2017-year-review-china%E2%80%99s-fresh-garlic-exports. Accessed on October 01, 2018.

SFGate. (2014). *Illegal Chinese garlic imports pounding U.S. industry 14 April 2014*. Retrieved from https://www.sfgate.com/news/article/Illegal-Chinese-garlic-imports-pounding-U-S-5396865.php. Accessed on October 01, 2018.

Sky News. (2018). Thai military called in to halt garlic smuggling. *Sky News*, May 31. Retrieved from https://news.sky.com/story/thai-military-called-in-to-halt-garlic-smuggling-11390632. Accessed on October 01, 2018.

Sveriges Radio. (2010). *Man tried to smuggle in 28 tons garlic*, 20 July 2010. Retrieved from https://sverigesradio.se/sida/artikel.aspx?programid=2054&artikel=3871620. Accessed on March 14, 2018.

UN Comtrade Database. (2018). Online trade statistics. Retrieved from https://comtrade.un.org/. Accessed on October 01, 2018.

World Bank. (2014). An evaluation of the EU-Turkey Custom Union, Report No. 85830-TR, WB: Washington. Accessed on March 14, 2018.

WSJ. (2000). Beijing–Seoul feud over garlic imports may be preview of future trade wars. *WSJ*, June 28. Retrieved from https://www.wsj.com/articles/SB962128531955216594. Accessed on March, 2018.

# PART II

## BREXIT THEMES

# 7

# THE IMPACT OF BREXIT ON THE CITY OF LONDON

## *Sir Mark Boleat*

## INTRODUCTION

Brexit will have profound effects on the financial services industry in the UK, commonly although somewhat misleadingly referred to as 'the City of London'. Those effects will not be known for many years, largely because the nature of the future relationship between Britain and the EU is not yet known and may well not be known for some time. Even when it is known it will take some years for the market to fully adjust, at a time when many other factors will also be influencing the evolution of financial services markets.

This chapter takes the position as at September 2018, after the publication of 'the Chequers plan', but well before any final agreement between Britain and the EU27. The current 'best guess' is that Britain will leave the European Union on 29 March 2019, but with a transitional period until the end of 2020 during which time nothing will change. From the beginning of 2021, Britain will be a 'third country' in respect of financial services, with no special access to the EU Single Market. But financial institutions have to be ready to cope with a range of possibilities from 'crashing out' in March 2019 with no transitional period, through to an extended transitional period to the unlikely, but still possible, Britain not leaving the EU. The range of possibilities, and the long lead time for some financial institutions in making location decisions, is itself having an effect on the City of London, regardless of the outcome.

## WHAT DO WE MEAN BY THE 'CITY OF LONDON'

The term 'City of London' or, more commonly 'the City' is used to mean a number of different things:

- The part of London for which the City of London Corporation is responsible, also known as 'the square mile'. The City Corporation itself has a representative role but which relates to the wider City not just the square mile, the area within which many of the major financial institutions are based.

- The financial services industry in London, including the other major centres of Canary Wharf and to some extent the West End, each of which is now home to many major financial institutions.

- The financial services industry in the UK, more particularly the wholesale markets. While most of this business is based in London, much of the activity is carried on outside London. For example, most of the large investment banks have a significant presence in other parts of the UK – JP Morgan in Bournemouth, Citi Group in Belfast, Deutsche Bank in Birmingham and Morgan Stanley in Glasgow.

- The international financial services industry, wherever it is based.

- Financial markets as in daily BBC news reports 'today in the City share prices increased modestly…'.

For the most part, this chapter is about the third definition but with a passing nod to the others. The central theme of this chapter is that the financial services industry, globally and in Europe, will be fine after Brexit, but a smaller proportion of it will be located in the UK. The key questions are how much smaller and over what period.

## WHY BREXIT IS IMPORTANT TO THE CITY

To set the scene, it is necessary to understand the importance of Brexit to the City. London is the world's leading international financial centre. It has achieved this status through a combination of factors – the rule of law, the English language, geographical location and an open society among others.

Most of the financial services industry in Britain is purely domestic. Businesses authorised and regulated in Britain, even if foreign owned, offer a wide range of financial services to people and corporates in Britain. For this part of the industry whether Britain is in the EU or not is largely irrelevant, given that there is no expectation of any significant divergence from EU standards, which in turn are influenced by global standards, following Britain's departure from the EU.

But a significant proportion of the industry based in Britain is international in nature, serving corporates, governments and people throughout the world. This sector of the market is to a significant extent, but not wholly, dependent on Britain being in the European Single Market, which covers almost all financial services. So, for example, a bank or an insurance company based in one member state can provide its services throughout the European Economic Area (EEA-the EU countries plus Iceland, Norway and Liechtenstein) without the need to establish separate businesses, with their own capital, liquidity and management, in each member state. This gives scope for significant economies of scale. Many international financial service businesses have taken advantage of this to centralise operations in a single state. The UK has been the principal beneficiary, although Dublin and Luxembourg have also benefited to some extent. Just a few statistics illustrate the point (TheCityUK, 2018):

- The UK had a financial services trade surplus of £68 billion in 2017, much higher than any other country. £18.5 billion of this surplus was with the EU27.

- The UK accounts for 37% of international foreign exchange trading, 39% of over-the-counter-interest-rate derivatives trading and 16% of cross-border bank lending.

- The UK financial services industry paid £72.1 billion in tax in 2016/17, 11% of the UK's total tax revenue.

For the avoidance of doubt, no other economic grouping of countries allows such cross-border activity; indeed, some countries, including the USA, restrict some businesses to operating within individual states. So, the US investment banks operating throughout the EU are not doing so through businesses established, capitalised, authorised and regulated in New York, but rather through businesses established, capitalised, authorised and regulated in London.

## THE POLICY DEBATE ON BREXIT AND FINANCIAL SERVICES

In June 2016, Britain voted to leave the European Union. However, it did not vote, and was not asked to vote, on where it was going. Two years on we were little the wiser. True, there is a leaving date, which can be varied, of 29 March 2019, political agreement, but not one that is legally certain, for a transitional period up to the end of 2020, and now an emerging view that Britain is not going to leave the customs union until a few years after 2020. However, there is still no clarity on the end-game. A 'deep and special relationship', 'frictionless trade' and 'leaving the Single Market and the customs union' are all government policies, but they are not compatible.

TheCityUK, the overall representative body for the financial services industry, set out its key 'ask' for the Brexit negotiations in January 2017 (TheCityUK, 2017). This was a bespoke agreement delivering mutual market access, transitional arrangements to allow for enough time to implement the new relationship and access to talent.

The concept of mutual market access, based on agreement to recognise that regulatory regimes, while different, can produce similar outcomes and with a dispute resolution mechanism, was explained in detail in a report by the International Regulatory Strategy Group with the support of the law firm Hogan Lovells (IRSG, 2017). The concept was at one stage embraced by the government, not surprising as it did not offend either of the two competing viewpoints on Brexit in the Cabinet. The Prime Minister announced support for the concept in her Mansion House speech (May, 2018) in January 2018. The Chancellor, in a speech (Hammond, 2018) on 7 March 2018, set out the UK's position in more detail:

> *But the principle of mutual recognition and reciprocal regulatory equivalence, provided it is objectively assessed, with proper governance structures, dispute resolution mechanisms, and sensible notice periods to market participants clearly could provide an effective basis for such a partnership.*

These proposals would preserve the benefits of efficient wholesale financial markets, serving corporates and governments throughout the EU. But they run into political realities.

They would to a large extent result in the UK having the benefit of being in the Single Market and would mark a significant departure from the principles on which the EU operates. It would actually put Britain in a more favourable position outside the EU than the member states inside would have. The reaction from the EU27 was not favourable, and there was never any chance that the EU27 would agree to it.

Sir Ivan Rogers, Britain's former ambassador to the EU, in a speech (Rogers, 2018) in May 2018, explained why the British proposal would not fly:

> So here, the UK is again advancing a proposition – snappily entitled bespoke dynamic mutual recognition – which has considerable substantive merits on how issues might be best ordered across international boundaries between regulators and supervisors on either side of the Channel, but is inevitably going to be rejected – indeed, already has been unequivocally rejected – as legally unviable. One cannot take oneself outside the jurisdiction of the ECJ, and leave the Single Market, and simultaneously demand a role that no non-member has in the shaping of EU regulation.
>
> Why, again, should members, who have painfully agreed an extremely detailed constraining single rule book, allow a non-member greater latitude than they have themselves to achieve so-called comparable regulatory outcomes – and agree a non-ECJ unique resolution mechanism to decide whether they are comparable? This is not going to happen in a month of Sundays.

The EU's position was that Britain will become a 'third country' after Brexit, with access to the Single Market through existing equivalence regime procedures. These provide for the EU Commission to certify that the regulatory regime in another jurisdiction produces equivalent outcomes to that of the EU, and therefore institutions based in that jurisdiction can do business in the Single Market. The industry was agreed that this equivalence regime was not the answer. The main reason is simply that it covers less than one-third of financial services and does not include mainstream banking and insurance. Also, in practice, the process of granting or withholding equivalence is political as much as technical.

The Government's preferred option did not last long. At its meeting at Chequers in July 2018 the British Government finally reached agreement on its preferred option for the long-term arrangement. Broadly speaking, this envisaged Britain remaining in the Single Market and customs union (in practice the government prefers that those actual words are not used) for goods but not for services. It came as a surprise to many that the government chose to prioritise goods rather than services, which are a much larger part of the economy. However, politically, it is easy to see why the government came to this view. What would be unacceptable would be shortages of medicines, empty shelves on the supermarkets, car production halting because of disrupted supply chains and chaos at Dover, with vivid TV pictures. By contrast, the effect on services would be less visible. This is partly because the Single Market in services is much less complete than that for goods and partly because for many services – tourism, public administration and education for example – the Single Market is irrelevant. For financial services the government took the view that the industry was capable of adapting to being outside the Single Market in a way that would not be noticed by anyone outside the industry and which certainly would not lead to damaging pictures on TV. That there would in the long term be a cost to the country in terms of lost employment and tax revenue was, in political terms, immaterial to a government fighting to stay in power in the short term.

The government's detailed proposals on financial services were set out in the post-Chequers White Paper (DEXEU, 2018):

> 64. This new economic and regulatory arrangement would be based on the principle of autonomy for each party over decisions regarding access to its market, with a bilateral framework of treaty-based commitments to underpin the operation of the relationship, ensure transparency and stability, and promote cooperation. Such an arrangement would respect the regulatory autonomy of both parties, while ensuring decisions made by either party are implemented in line with agreed processes, and that provision is made for necessary consultation and collaboration between the parties.

> 65. As part of this, the existing autonomous frameworks for equivalence would need to be expanded, to reflect the fact that equivalence as it exists today is not sufficient in scope for the breadth of the interconnectedness of UK-EU financial services provision. A new arrangement would need to encompass a broader range of cross-border activities that reflect global financial business models and the high degree of economic integration. The UK recognises, however, that this arrangement cannot replicate the EU's passporting regime.

> 66. As the UK and the EU start from a position of identical rules and entwined supervisory frameworks, the UK proposes that there should be reciprocal recognition of equivalence under all existing third

*country regimes, taking effect at the end of the implementation period. This reflects the reality that all relevant criteria, including continued supervisory cooperation, can readily be satisfied by both the UK and the EU. It would also provide initial confidence in the system to firms and markets.*

*67. Although future determinations of equivalence would be an autonomous matter for each party, the new arrangement should include provisions through the bilateral arrangement for:*

*a.   common principles for the governance of the relationship;*

*b.   extensive supervisory cooperation and regulatory dialogue; and*

*c.   predictable, transparent and robust processes.*

In short, the Government accepted that the future relationship would be based on equivalence but with the wish for this to be enhanced through enhanced co-operation. There is little expectation that such enhancement will be forthcoming; indeed there is pressure from some countries to make the current equivalence procedures more onerous.

## WHAT THE INDUSTRY HAS DONE IN ANTICIPATION OF BREXIT

While the policy debate rages on business has simply got on with it, preparing for a worst-case scenario as it is prudent to do. The contingency plans were drafted long ago; they are now in the implementation stage.

Each financial services business that operates in other countries in the EEA – and even some that do not – has had to plan for Brexit. Financial services businesses are heavily regulated, have demanding customers, and many engage in long-term transactions. They are expected to manage risks intensively.

There is clearly a non-negligible risk that from 29 March 2019 Britain will no longer be in the European Union or the Single Market, and that there will be restrictions on labour movement between the other EEA countries and the UK. This risk has to be mitigated. Following the agreement on 'sufficient progress' at the European Council in December 2017 it now seems probable that the UK will remain in the Single Market until the end of 2020 at least. But this is not bankable. There can be no certainty that it will be implemented until the UK's withdrawal agreement has been ratified, which will not happen, if it happens, until early 2019. More generally, the value of transitional arrangements diminishes by the day. If they are finally agreed in March 2019 that will be too late for most institutions, although some might be able to slowdown restructuring of their business.

Two side-effects of Brexit planning work have become apparent:

- Business now sees the costs, as well as the benefits, of concentrating activity in one location. More generally, Britain's reputation as having a stable political, economic and regulatory environment for international business has significantly diminished, which will have an impact regardless of the final Brexit outcome.

- Some of the work on location should have been done anyway, and even with a favourable Brexit outcome some businesses will see merit in moving some business from the UK for economic reasons – for all of its attractions, Britain, and London particularly, is a high-cost place to do business. And, related to this, once location is on the agenda it is not confined to the issue that caused it to be on the agenda. Businesses will look at their location policy, in some cases immediately, in others in the longer term.

The two factors reinforce each other.

For the most part businesses are, in the short term, doing the minimum to provide continuity of service to their customers; what this is depends on the nature of the business and the method of operation of the individual company. It also depends on the attitude of regulators in the EU27 and in the UK. Regulators in the EU27 will not accept firms establishing 'letter box companies', with all business continuing to be done from the UK. This type of arrangement is not acceptable to any regulator – including the Prudential Regulation Authority in the UK. Regulators require capital, liquidity and management to be in the jurisdiction in which the business is authorised. However, regulators recognise the exceptional circumstances that Brexit presents – with many institutions trying to do the same thing at the same time, which itself poses resource problems for the regulators. Accordingly, they are taking a pragmatic approach, accepting a limited transfer of functions initially but with the stipulation that over a period of three to five years all the required functions will be transferred. So, this might mean, for example, 50 staff initially but 500 after three years.

The impression is sometimes given that there is one button that all financial institutions will press at roughly the same time to shift some of their operations to other centres in the EEA. This is not the case. Financial services businesses are affected by Brexit in very different ways even if they are doing similar business. Most financial services businesses have been going through a series of steps to make their plans from an initial scoping exercise covering what business must be moved through to analysing workarounds and other short-term options, analysis of longer term options and then the expensive work of a comprehensive analysis of new locations, obtaining the necessary consents and then the really expensive work of implementation.

It is impossible to give a precise estimate of the extent of relocation activity so far as a result of Brexit. Most businesses are not issuing press releases saying what they are doing; they are just doing it. Following is a summary of what some of the larger financial institutions have done:

- Barclays bank is moving some business to Dublin.

- RBS is building up its operation in Amsterdam.

- Standard Chartered is establishing its EU business in Frankfurt.

- Lloyds banking group has chosen Berlin as its EU base.

- HSBC is building on its existing business in Paris.

- Goldman Sachs has moved client-facing people to Milan, Paris and Frankfurt and has reported that 'no one has turned down a Brexit-inspired move'.

- Wells Fargo is planning to use Paris and Dublin as post-Brexit hubs.

- Bank of America Merrill Lynch has similarly opted for Paris and Dublin.

- JP Morgan is enlarging its business in Dublin and will also be relocating staff to Frankfurt.

- Morgan Stanley is building up its businesses in Frankfurt and Paris.

- UBS has chosen Frankfurt as its main EU base.

- EY has reported that 39% of wealth and asset management firms have publicly said that they are moving some operations out of the UK – to Dublin and Luxembourg.

- Bloomberg is moving its EU trading operations from London to Amsterdam.

- Thomson Reuters is moving its foreign exchange derivatives trading from London to Dublin.

- Lloyds of London has established a subsidiary in Brussels.

These moves are bad for London – but they are also bad for the EU as by increasing costs without increasing business and reducing economies of scale they will make financial markets less efficient. However, they are not sufficiently bad to have a significant influence on the EU position, particularly as several EU states see the benefit to them of having a larger financial services industry.

## THE IMPACT OF BREXIT ON THE CITY

So, what has been the overall impact of Brexit on the City so far?

Brexit has already had a significant impact, although most of this impact is not easy to see. Even though Britain will be outside the EU it will be affected by EU policies. In particular, those financial institutions that wish to operate within the EEA post-Brexit will have to comply with EU rules. It follows that being able to influence those rules is important, particularly as Britain dominates the European wholesale financial markets. The UK has been very successful at influencing EU regulation over the last 30 years through a combination of expertise that goes with the size and importance of the industry, excellent work by officials in the Treasury and regulatory bodies, good input from the industry by individual companies and trade associations, and excellent work by a small number of Members of the European Parliament.

Immediately after the referendum this influence has diminished as there is less capacity, and indeed willingness, for Britain to have an influence and less willingness to give British views the same weight as they previously had.

A second factor has been the diversion of resources away from strategy and product development to dealing with Brexit. Large project teams have been put in place in major companies, aided by consultancy and legal support. So, staff who were previously working on expanding the business are now working on protecting existing business. This will not show through in aggregate figures but will be apparent in profit and loss accounts. Major banks have individually spent over £100 million on Brexit plans and the cumulative costs runs into billions – the Boston Consulting Group has estimated (Boston Consulting Group, 2017) that 'the cost of restructuring could be as much as €15 billion'. Similar figures are reported in the other sectors most affected by Brexit – chemicals, pharmaceuticals and the motor industry. In its annual report GSK (GSK, 2018) has estimated transitional costs of £70 million and ongoing costs of £50 million a year. None of this is productive.

It is very likely that new investment has been reduced, though it is almost impossible to give precise examples. Decisions that might have been to expand or to set up in Britain were deferred or even cancelled. Equally, as outlined in the previous section, businesses have been building up their operations in other EEA centres in anticipation of Brexit. All these decisions have been at the margin, perhaps affecting anything between a few jobs and 100 jobs at a time, but cumulatively they are significant.

Accordingly, the effect on employment so far has been comparatively small, and largely reflects new jobs not being created. For the most part the new offices in the EU27 are employing additional staff rather than taking staff from London and other parts of the UK. TheCityUK has estimated that the total effect so far is a net loss of around 10,000 jobs.

## THE LONG-TERM IMPACT

The longer-term impact of Brexit on the financial services industry in the UK is unknown. It depends primarily on the final exit agreement between Britain and the EU. This may include some useful mitigating measures such as grandfathering clauses which will facilitate a more orderly shift of business from the UK to other centres but which, for the reasons already stated, will give nothing like the current level of market access.

The alternative scenarios were analysed in a report by the Oliver Wyman consultancy (Oliver Wyman, 2017). It concluded that if the UK retained market access on near to current terms the impact would be only modest, with 3,000–4,000 jobs at risk and tax revenue falling by less than £500 million a year. At the other end of the spectrum, if the UK had no special status with the EU – now the most likely option – the industry would lose £18–20 billion a year in revenue, which would put 31,000–35,000 jobs at risk along with £3–5 billion a year of tax revenue. There would also be a knock-on impact on the ecosystem that could result in the loss from the UK of activities that operate alongside those parts of the business that leave, the shifting of entire business units or the closure of lines of business due to increased costs. An estimated further £14–18 billion of revenue, 34,000–40,000 jobs and £5 billion in tax revenue per annum might be at risk. So, the worst-case scenario – which currently looks to be the most likely – is the loss of 75,000 jobs and £10 billion of tax revenue.

Jamie Dimon, CEO of JP Morgan, has summarised the position well in his most recent annual letter to shareholders (Dimon, 2018), published in April 2018.

> *We have the resources to be prepared for a hard Brexit, as we must be. It essentially means moving 300–400 jobs around Europe in the short term and modifying some of our legal entities to be able to conduct business the day after Brexit. What we do not know — and will not know until the negotiations are complete — is what the end state will look like. Although unlikely, there is the possibility that we could stay exactly as we are today. Unfortunately, the worst outcome would be much of London's financial center moving to the Continent over time. We hope for all involved that this outcome will not be the case.*

This comment is usefully supplemented by evidence by Mark Garvin, UK country head of JP Morgan in evidence to a House of Commons committee (Garvin, 2018) in September 2018:

> *We began our planning in August of 2016. We are now in full execution mode. We are in the very last stages of execution, in fact. A number of these initiatives are already in flight. In many cases, we have passed the point of no return. They are happening. Our intention is to migrate our commercial banking and to merge our wealth management business, the EU-focused businesses, into our Luxembourg bank. Those plans are already being enacted.*
>
> *The JPMorgan AG Frankfurt bank will be the domicile that will be hosting our investment banking and markets business. That will take*

*longer. It is more complex. Those two banks will be branching out across the EU-27 countries. We are not going to a single location; we are going to a more distributive model than we have had in the past.*

Howard Davies has similarly distinguished between the long and the short term. In an article in *Financial World* (Davies, 2018) he notes that when Britain leaves the EU 'those who are keen on localisation than on global markets will be in the ascendant'. He notes in particular the adverse effect on London if the right to delegate fund management outside the EU was withdrawn or Euro-clearing was pulled back to the Eurozone. In a timely analogy he comments that this is a long game – 'we are still early in the first half, and the final result is impossible to call'.

## CONCLUSIONS

The conclusions from this analysis are clear. The financial services industry, quite properly, is preparing for the worst possible Brexit outcome – no special access to the EU market from March 2019. Accordingly, functions and a small number of people are being moved from London to other EU centres. Other than some real issues on the continuity of existing contracts, particularly insurance and derivatives, the financial services industry will take Brexit in its stride such that customers and the media will scarcely notice – certainly compared with the chaos that may appear in other sectors. But business is being, and will continue to be, lost to Britain will resultant effects on employment and tax revenue. The full impact will not be felt for many years – until the final Brexit outcome is not only agreed but is firmly established. Other factors will play a part, in particular domestic policies on tax, regulation and migration. The financial markets in London – one definition of 'the City' – will remain large and vibrant but less so than would be the case if Britain remained in the EU. Britain will lose influence in international fora and is destined to become more of a rule-taker than a rule-setter. Brexit will do damage to the City, however defined. Compensating domestic policies could mitigate the damage but as yet there is little sign that this will happen.

## REFERENCES

Boston Consulting Group. (2017). *Bridging to Brexit: Insights from European SMEs, Corporates and Investors.* Report commissioned by AFME.

DEXEU. (2018). The future relationship between the United Kingdom and the European Union, Cmnd 9593, July 2018.

Davies. (2018, June/July). Sir Howard Davies, Brexit: A game of two halves. *Financial World.*

Dimon. (2018). *Jamie Dimon, Chairman and CEO letter to Shareholders.* Annual report 2017. JP Morgan Chase & Co.

Garvin (2018). Mark Garvin, Vice Chairman, JP Morgan Corporate and Investment Bank, oral evidence to Treasury Committee on The UK's economic relationship with the European Union, HC 473, 11 September 2018.

GSK. (2018). *GSK Annual report 2017.*

Hammond. (2018, March 7). Philip Hammond. Chancellor's HSBC speech: Financial services.

IRSG. (2017). A new basis for access to EU/UK financial services post-Brexit.

May. (2018). *Theresa May*. PM speech on our future economic partnership with the European Union, 2 March.

Oliver Wyman. (2017). The impact of the UK's exit from the EU on the UK-based financial services sector.

Rogers. (2018). Sir Ivan Rogers. Blog: The real post Brexit options – lecture. Policy Scotland, 23 May.

TheCityUK. (2017). Brexit and UK-based financial and professional services.

TheCityUK. (2018, April). Key facts about UK-based financial and related professional services.

# 8

# BREXIT AND THE POTENTIAL BUSINESS IMPACT ON ENGLISH SMES

*Vicky Pryce, Beverley Nielsen and Steven McCabe*

## INTRODUCTION

This chapter considers the way Brexit has impacted SMEs involved in production supply chains in general and in the West Midlands in particular. It is important to remember that SMEs are an essential part of the trading environment, accounting for 99% of businesses and 60% of private sector employment in UK (Rhodes, 2017), and are essential to the supply chain of major businesses including Original Equipment Manufacturers (OEMs) whose exports are vital to economic success.

The focus here is on how these factors and a range of possible interventions might support productivity and competitiveness and in turn counter the impacts of Brexit on the West Midlands and other English Regions in the UK. As such, three sections are presented:

1.  Disentangling the UK Government's attitude to business during Brexit negotiations.
2.  How are businesses coping with Brexit?
3.  What business support might government offer to SMEs?

## DISENTANGLING THE UK GOVERNMENT'S ATTITUDE TO BUSINESS DURING BREXIT NEGOTIATIONS

Unsurprisingly, since the referendum in June 2016, business organisations have asked for as much clarity as possible in terms of the UK's negotiating position and its potential impact on their members. There have been tangible economic consequences including the fall of the pound, making imports more expensive whilst also reducing the relative price of goods for export. Economic data demonstrate tightening living standards as incomes have failed to match the increased prices of goods imported, especially food, with consequences for UK growth rates, expected to slow to 1.3% in 2018 (Pricewaterhouse-Coopers, 2018), far below the rate in 2014–2015 and its slowest since the recession of 2009 (Office for National Statistics, 2018). More worryingly, the primary consequence of Brexit on business has been the impact of uncertainty in reducing confidence levels and hitting investment intentions. Instead of continuing to rise by between 6% and 10% annually, business investment fell in first quarter 2018 by 0.2% (Smith, 2018).

Whilst attention has inevitably been focussed on big businesses, there is a sense that the concerns of smaller businesses have been overlooked. SMEs account for 99% of all businesses, and employ over 16 million people representing 60% of the total of all private sector employees of 26.7 million employed by firms in the UK (Rhodes, 2017). Though not all of these businesses import or export to the EU, in 2016 a report by the Department for Business Innovation & Skills, assessing the proportion of SMEs in the supply chains of exporters, estimated that 9% of UK SMEs export and a further 15% are in the supply chains of other exporting businesses. Using only registered businesses, the proportion of SMEs exporting was 10% and the proportion in supply chains was 17%. For the business population as a whole, 78% of exporters exported to the EU (Department for Business Innovation and Skills, 2016).

In contrast to the much-vaunted success of Germany's *Mittelstand*, UK SMEs, whilst continuing to employ generations from the same families and investing for the long term, often through retained earnings, tend not to generate interest amongst the media. This is despite the fact that many of these firms actively engage in incremental or radical product innovations providing value through the supply chain allowing major manufacturers to enjoy success in terms of high-quality products, many of which are exported.

In a survey carried out by IDEA of its Growth Panel members in late 2017, it was found that over a quarter of those surveyed generated over 40% of their revenues from new products launched in the past three years (Nielsen, 2017). They felt overlooked without sufficient means for formal communications, echoing concerns raised by Lord Heseltine in 'No Stone Unturned', calling for 'enhanced roles' for Chambers of Commerce and Local Enterprise Partnerships (Heseltine, 2012). Small businesses face particular challenges in preparing for Brexit:

> *Some are getting ready for it to reduce economic damage. Some won't prepare because they're hoping for a deal. But in reality many firms can't prepare because the cost of change is simply too high to even consider it .... To those whose first and only choice is for Britain to walk away without a deal, I say you're not only wrong but irresponsible. (CBI, 2017)*

Just as SMEs in general can struggle to make their voices heard, regional businesses face particular challenges. The contribution of manufacturing to the national economy is, at 10%, a shadow of what it once was in the 1970s. However, in the British Midlands in 2017 manufacturing accounted for 16% of output (Office for National Statistics, 2017). Significantly, exports have increased dramatically over the past decade, with a high dependence on integrated supply chains (Forrest et al., 2017). Clearly, any circumstances that potentially undermined this ability to trade effectively was a cause of considerable concern for all involved.

As such, it is not surprising that government analysis predicts that a hard Brexit would hit the North East, West Midlands and Northern Ireland particularly hard due to, in the case of the first two regions, dependence on motor manufacturing and in Northern Ireland, reliance with Southern Ireland, most particularly, agriculture and allied sectors (House of Commons, 2018). This will undoubtedly pose significant challenges to many SMEs.

## HOW ARE BUSINESSES COPING WITH BREXIT?

The actions taken by the coalition government elected in 2010 through austerity budgets led to significant cuts to the Department for Business, Innovation and Skills. This, in turn, led to the abolition in 2012 of the Regional Development Agencies in England, the Business Link service in 2011, The Business Growth Service (BGS), including the Manufacturing Advisory Service (MAS), and closure in 2015 of the Growth Accelerator programme. The effect was to undermine the ability of SMEs to access advice and to some degree finance. A survey carried out by IDEA in 2017 discovered that SMEs felt that their needs in terms of effective business support systems and financial aid were not being adequately recognised and addressed (Nielsen, 2017). In the period since the referendum vote of June 2016, SMEs in England have experienced a paucity of advice and guidance as to what they should do. One IDEA Growth Panel SME manufacturer commented that

> *It was catastrophic and foolish to lose our business support infrastructure. We feel that people in government are only now realising that these were good mechanisms for contacting local businesses and in particular SMEs. (Nielsen, 2017)*

In contrast, the devolved nations had not seen such dramatic shifts in business support infrastructure. Enterprise Northern Ireland was established in 2000; the Scottish Development Agency in 1975, later becoming Scottish Enterprise in 1991; the Welsh Development Agency set up in 1976, had become part of the Welsh government in 2006 and was delivering the Business Wales programme.

In the devolved nations SMEs were receiving grant support, with the Scottish Government announcing a 100% grant of up to £4,000 in June 2018, available through Scottish Development International (SDI) (Scottish Cabinet Office, 2018). InterTradeIreland made vouchers worth up to £2,000 available for legal or other specialist advice about Brexit. In the Republic, an Enterprise Ireland website provided businesses with links to research, a scorecard with Q&A functions and €5,000 grants.

In January 2018, a study by the University of St Andrews, using UK government data covering approximately 10,000 SMEs, investigated which SMEs were most concerned by Brexit and the likely impact of this on their future strategic intentions relating to finance, growth, innovation and capital expenditure. Results showed that larger, innovative, export-oriented SMEs and those operating in business services saw

Brexit as a major obstacle to business success. Regression-based analysis suggested Brexit could lead to weaker growth, lower levels of innovation, reduced capital investment and lower access to external finance, especially for innovative and export-oriented SMEs. Importantly, Brexit was perceived as having the most significant negative repercussions for the SMEs often viewed as the largest contributors to long-term productivity growth (Brown, Liñares Zegarra, & Wilson, 2018). In February 2018, Moore Stephens' survey of owner-managed businesses found that 94% of 653 owner-managed businesses surveyed felt government was ignoring their concerns over Brexit (Lamb, 2018).

Moreover, a survey conducted by IDEA of its Growth Panels in March 2018 consisting of almost 70 West Midlands SMEs in construction, energy and transport sectors, showed confidence levels had been impacted by Brexit fears and that whilst 10% of firms were more confident, 50% were less confident, with 40% feeling the same. Of those exporting 25% were doing better, 50% worse and 25% about the same. For those importing raw materials, prices had increased hitting margins and leading to price increases, with further rises anticipated. For firms in automotive supply chains there was considerable concern regarding disruption over potential tariffs (see also Chapter 9 in this book), with one manufacturer outlining his fears over costs, stating

> *If that becomes an issue it may well be cheaper to import certain items from China rather than the EU, which is something we don't want to do as we look to support local sourcing and work with long-term trading partners within the EU.*

In speaking about Brexit preparations, a typical response was that,

> *We're not sure how much we can do as we are not*
> *sure what deal will be done, if a deal will be done*
> *at all. We are going on a course to see what trade*
> *benefits there are with Canada.*

Another participant reflected on the situation in their company:

> *We carried out a Risk assessment on our company,*
> *which we do every year and we are constantly*
> *looking at risks across the business. Because we are*
> *a small company we have to run our company. But*
> *here we don't really know what the end game will*
> *be. We are planning for world trade rules which will*
> *be damaging for the UK car industry with knock on*
> *impacts for smaller suppliers.*

Few companies were aware of the impacts of changes to third country partners. As a participant in the survey believed,

> *With our raw material being a world traded*
> *commodity I am not clear if I would be affected*
> *if I am buying from Scandinavia and we have not*
> *considered this yet.*

Moreover, as the following comments strongly indicate, there is widespread belief that the UK Government does not fully understood the widespread implications for the West Midlands economy:

> *They have a very narrow view based on Jaguar*
> *Land Rover, but have no regard for SMEs.*

> *It's very worrying because why throw a spanner*
> *in the works when you don't have to. If everyone*
> *knew what they know now they would not vote for*
> *Brexit again.*

*Yes, I am worried. So easy for people to phone up and come over with a lorry and take products. If that's going to be delayed in ports and customs, it will disrupt trade. Can't see it being very slick and backlogs of lorries will be an issue.*

*I do think we will be hit as they are predicting. Areas more strongly opposed to staying in the EU are going to be poorer areas that will be more badly hit. I think what they say will affect a lot of businesses and a lot of people will be affected jobwise.*

The survey demonstrated that there were three critical and immediate issues of concern to business following Brexit:

1. Skills shortages and employment losses.
2. Lower investment levels.
3. Falling UK sales due to reduced incomes.

These issues could be contrasted against three reasons for optimism following Brexit identified by respondents, although with longer timescales anticipated in terms of likely impacts:

1. Increased policy focus on import substitution and global trade.
2. EU reforms within the EU stimulated through Brexit.
3. Opportunity for tariff controls on imports from outside the EU leading to greater price competitiveness for UK-produced goods.

A British Chamber of Commerce (BCC) survey of 2,500 firms released in September 2018 showed that 62% of firms still had not completed any Brexit risk assessment. A fifth stated they would cut their investment if there was no deal, with 20% planning to move their business to the EU in this scenario, whilst a further 18% aimed to cut back on recruitment. However, these numbers declined dramatically in the event of a status quo transition. Demonstrating the gaps in preparations between larger and smaller companies the figures showed 69% of micros (9 and under employees) not having completed any assessment, compared to 24% of businesses with over 250 employees. Many firms were either awaiting greater clarity, or were suffering from 'Brexit fatigue'. To help firms consider the large range of variants involved, the BCC had prepared a checklist helping companies to plan ahead although no government grant funding was available to firms in England (BCC, 2018).

The findings from the BCC are that businesses generally remain ill-prepared, with few prepared at all, and with next to no resource directed to supporting them from government or other agencies, a feature which has characterised the Brexit process up to the point of writing. Firms that are hard pressed in maintaining existing business simply do not have resources to divert towards planning for an outcome that is uncertain. Grant Thornton's Quarterly Economic Briefing published in July 2018 contained the warning that with the likelihood of a no deal Brexit increasing, "Uncertainty remains and that will continue for some time. Organisations should do scenario planning and have contingency plans in place if they have not done so already." However, evidence from discussions had with those engaged in business demonstrates that few have contingency plans with most working on a 'wait to see what happens' approach and dealing with the implications and consequences as they occur. Whilst those we have spoken to stress that this far from ideal, they contend that this is the only practical option given the huge range of possibilities facing them.

Though it is the views of large manufacturers that has gar-
nered headlines, smaller firms based in the Midlands' supply-
chains, vital to the continued success of such large firms, have
no less concern about the potential impact of Brexit. EEF and
CBI members have highlighted the demands of additional
paperwork requirements for Customs Declarations forms,
Rules of Origin, gaining Authorised Economic Operator status – a process which could take up to six months, worker
registration systems requiring greater clarity around day trips
to the EU in light of varying definitions of 'postings', and 'settled status', especially as applied to those in mixed marriages.

By late 2018, IDEA Growth Panel firms were expressing
even greater concerns over the situation confronting them as
the chances of no deal increased:

> *How can we as business people know what to do if
> we don't know what's agreed and not agreed. There
> is some potential for us in stocking more materials
> and contacting our customers as lower tier suppliers
> to suggest they too stock extra product. But we
> feel nervous about this as they might think about
> moving tools away from the UK and this would
> damage our business.*

> *For us as a business, as we have seen the drop in net
> EU migrant workers falling from 320k to 100k, we
> have found it much harder to appoint people into
> jobs. People are not coming to the UK as much.
> Poles that are here are largely assimilated, but the
> younger ones are not coming over. Our wages are
> not going up as much as the rest of the EU – at
> around 7–8% in Czech Republic and Poland,
> compared to 2.5% in UK.*

BMW, employing 8,000 people across four plants in the UK, believes that delays to components for Mini and Rolls-Royce cars caused by Brexit would force it to cease production in the UK (O'Carroll, 2018). The knock-on impacts would have a profound impact on thousands of workers employed in businesses in the Midlands employed in the supply chain (O'Carroll& Topham, 2018).

BMW's concerns are echoed by Dr Ralf Speth, CEO Jaguar Land Rover (JLR), a company employing 40,000 workers directly and 260,000 workers indirectly in their supply chain. Speth has warned that a poor deal on Brexit that does not achieve easy access to the EU could jeopardise up to £80 billion of investments over the next five years. It is estimated that the additional tariffs of £2,700 per car exported would be the consequence of WTO rules and the additional costs and delays of components being imported from outside the UK would cut profit by £1.2 billion a year severely undermining its competitiveness (Jack, 2018). Worryingly, Speth has stated that in such a scenario JLR would consider leaving the UK despite have spent £50 billion in the UK over the past five years.

This is particularly challenging given the number of SMEs in the supply chain for each of these businesses. As such, it should be noted that what happens to OEMs will have a critical impact on their suppliers (especially through tiers 2, 3 and 4). Nissan claims to have been 'left in the dark and unable to plan' because of Brexit with CEO, Carlos Ghosn, arguing that

> *So far we have absolutely no clue how this is going to end up. I don't think any company can maintain its activity if it is not competitive … little by little you're going to have a decline. It may take some time, but you're going to have a decline. (Manning, 2018)*

Honda informed *The Financial Times* that it stores sufficient parts to keep its Civic production line in Swindon operating for just 36 hours. The fact that in order to operate for nine days would require a warehouse the size of 42 football pitches indicates how vulnerable such companies are to any potential disruption caused by Brexit (Baker & Campbell, 2018). In August 2018, Ford issued a warning stating it would take 'whatever action needed' to protect its business, blaming uncertainty over Brexit for a drop in its 2017 European earnings (Watts, 2018). CEO, McLaren Automotive, Mike Flewitt, added his concerns regarding a no-deal Brexit with Andy Palmer, CEO Aston Martin stating they had increased their stock of engine supplies from three to five days in preparation, with a shut-down being planned in the event of a no deal Brexit (BBC, 2018).

Given what has been described, it is no surprise that Mike Hawes, CEO, Society of Motor Manufacturers and Traders (SMMT), has felt compelled to issue warning after warning:

> *There is no Brexit dividend for our industry,*
> *particularly in what is an increasingly hostile*
> *and protectionist global trading environment.*
> *Our message to government is that until it can*
> *demonstrate exactly how a new model for customs*
> *and trade with the EU can replicate the benefits we*
> *currently enjoy, don't change it. (Holder, 2018)*

Aeronautical engineering faces similar concerns. Airbus employs 14,000 people at 25 sites across Britain supporting 100,000 supply chain jobs. With plans to stockpile parts being progressed, they pressed government regarding their urgent need for clarification with a no-deal scenario leading to 'catastrophic' consequences.

> *We are already beginning to press the button on our*
> *crisis actions … We have sought to highlight our*

*concerns over the past 12 months, without success.*
*Far from 'project fear', this is a dawning reality*
*for Airbus. Put simply, a no-deal scenario directly*
*threatens Airbus's future in the UK. (Greenfield, 2018)*

This begs answers to the question as to what business support should the government offer to SMEs to ameliorate the negative consequences of Brexit?

## WHAT BUSINESS SUPPORT MIGHT GOVERNMENT OFFER TO SMES?

The view that government could have done more to assist business is undoubtedly true. However, it is accepted that during the negotiation process Theresa May and her team have been politically constrained in achieving a deal that whilst faithful to the outcome of the June 2016 referendum vote to leave the EU, allows business to continue as seamlessly as possible.

The consequences of no deal have been described in previous sections as being potentially catastrophic for businesses of all sizes, though companies that trade internationally, being part of global supply chains especially in transport, life sciences, agrifoods or which rely on EU labour including health, hospitality and agriculture, will be especially hard hit. Communication is a key issue that has been raised with many lamenting the loss of former communications channels. As one manufacturer on the IDEA Growth Panel noted:

*DTI used to produce leaflets and send them to*
*businesses outlining what they were doing, helping*
*SMEs to feel involved. SMEs do not have a strong*
*lobbying voice speaking up for them; Business Link*
*and other services have been dismantled, Chambers*

*of Commerce are fragmented, CBI tends to focus
on the larger businesses and whilst we are a
member of the FSB, they represent one of so many
voices out there.*

It is something of an irony that, in February 2018, the
Institute for Government unequivocally stated that UK business seeking clarity as to what might occur in the event of
no deal being the outcome of negotiations 'would be better
off' seeking guidance from the EU through consultation of
25 documents produced by the European Commission in
order to better understand what might occur (Owen, 2018).
Nonetheless, there remain many who believe that the UK's
departure from the EU offers the opportunity for business to
develop new approaches.

In research carried out amongst over 100 SME companies
forming part of IDEA's 'Growth Panel' in late 2017, businesses in the West Midlands wanted to see a number of initiatives
implemented as part of the UK's departure from the EU, with
a focus on developing a regional business support system
to deliver skills, finance and connectivity required (Nielsen,
2017). Crucial issues highlighted included:

- Closer working between colleges, universities and business
  to produce skills for local industries.
- Focus on skills retention and more careers support in
  schools.
- Greater levels of industry and supply chain focussed
  support with circular economy and local sourcing seen as
  means to deliver inclusive growth; for example, delivering
  300k homes nationally using local materials would deliver
  £94 billion annually through recognised multiplier impacts.
- More insights into anticipated Brexit outcomes for
  automotive, aerospace and transport equipment
  manufacturing.

- Business involvement in the Brexit negotiations.
- Continuing to invest in essential infrastructure to deliver a 'Roosevelt-style' *Square Deal* for the English regions.
- Ensuring follow-through with the Industrial Strategy, Catapult Centres and Devolution of business support.
- Retaining compliance with European BS EN Standards, preferable to compliance with US standards, with concerns over Non-Tariff Barrier impacts.
- Retaining freedom of labour movements or linking immigration more to positive economic contributions as outlined in a more recent CBI report (Percival & Barrett, 2018).
- Retaining freedom of services movements.
- Kick-starting the economy through public–private sector collaborations enabling multiyear settlements for the public sector and driving investment into innovations.

With 46% of companies finding it difficult to access finance required to meet their planned growth proposals recommendations included:

- More asset financing and access to Innovate UK funding.
- Fewer funding guarantee requirements or more risk cover for exports and loans.
- Simplified grant funding through government or regional banking schemes or incentivising customers to invest in renewable energy schemes.

## CONCLUSION

This chapter has examined the potential impact of Brexit on English SMEs. A report published in mid-October 2018 by the Government's official independent economic forecaster, the Office for Budget Responsibility (OBR), expressed the view that Brexit had already negatively impacted on the UK economy. Growth was seen as having been reduced by between 2% and 2.5% compared to where it might have been due to lower household spending and business investment being held back because of uncertainty (OBR, 2018). Worryingly, the OBR asserted, the closest historical parallel to there being a 'no-deal Brexit' would be the 'Three-Day Week' of 1974 during which there was 3% reduction to the UK's GDP in one quarter alone. Clearly, it is abundantly apparent, the importance of getting a good outcome for business from Brexit negotiations is critical.

As Lord Bridges noted (House of Lords, 2017), Brexit requires the creation of a new partnership touching on every aspect of our lives, amounting, as he put it, to 'a gargantuan task'. For business, the uncertainty has eroded confidence to such levels that towards the end of 2018 business surveys showed optimism had slumped with fears over Brexit at highest levels yet, with business spending and hiring being expected to slow and further interest rate and inflationary increases anticipated for the coming year (Stewart, De Senior, Porter, & Simmons, 2018). Whilst business understood the Prime Minister's main constraint was her divided Cabinet and a divided country, with her main objective being to get consensus on a deal she could get through Parliament, no one was clear what it would mean after that. A great deal of energy would be expended getting a deal over the line but to what end, with an even greater task remaining and the growing fear that the uncertainty would go on for years.

## REFERENCES

Baker, A., & Campbell, P. (2018). Honda faces the real cost of Brexit in a former Spitfire Plant. CNBC website.

Accessed on June 29. Retrieved from https://www.cnbc.com/2018/06/27/honda-faces-the-real-cost-of-brexit-in-a-former-spitfire-plant.html

BBC. (2018). Andy Palmer, CEO, Aston Martin, speaking on Today Programme. Radio 4 Today Programme, 29 August.

British Chambers of Commerce (BCC). (2018). Six months to Brexit: Major new BCC survey finds investment and recruitment would be cut in event of `no deal' BCC website accessed 28th September. Retrieved from https://www.britishchambers.org.uk/news/2018/09/six-months-to-brexit-major-new-bcc-survey-finds-investment-and-recruitment-would-be-cut-in-the-event-of-no-deal.

Brown, R., Liñares Zegarra, J., & Wilson, J. (2018). *What happens if the rules change? The impact of Brexit on the future strategic intentions of UK SMEs.* Working Paper in Responsible Banking & Finance, Centre for Responsible Banking & Finance, School of Management, University of St Andrews.

CBI. (2017). WTO rules would open a Pandora's Box. CBI website announcement. Accessed on July 15, 2018.

Department for Business Innovation and Skills. (2016, May). UK SMEs in the supply chains of exporters to the EU, Methodology Note, Department for Business Innovation and Skills.

Forrest, P., Jones, R., Hearne, D., Forrest, M., Beer, J., Pearson, J., …, Crane, C. (2017). *Making a success of Brexit.* Retrieved from https://www.bcu.ac.uk/Download/Asset/be279cea-e7e3-e611-80c9-0050568319fd

Grant Thornton (2018), Quarterly Economic Briefing, July 2018, Retrieved from https://www.grantthornton.

co.uk/globalassets/1.-member-firms/united-kingdom/pdf/
documents/quarterly-economic-briefing-july-2018.pdf

Greenfield, P. (2018, June 22). Airbus plans UK job
cuts amid fears of hard Brexit impact. *The Guardian*.
website accessed 22nd June. Retrieved fromhttps://
www.theguardian.com/politics/2018/jun/22/
airbus-plans-uk-cuts-amid-fears-of-hard-brexit-impact

Heseltine, M. (2012). *No stone unturned, in pursuit of
growth*. Department for Business Innovation & Skills,
London. Retrieved from https://assets.publishing.service.
gov.uk/government/uploads/system/uploads/attachment_
data/file/34648/12-1213-no-stone-unturned-in-pursuit-of-
growth.pdf.

Holder, J. (2018). There is no Brexit dividend for the UK car
industry: Just risk warns automotive chief, *Autocar*. website
accessed 26th June. Retrieved from https://www.autocar.
co.uk/car-news/industry/there-no-brexit-dividend-uk-car-
industry-just-risk-warns-automotive-chief

House of Commons. (2018, January). *EU exit analysis
cross Whitehall Briefing*. House of Commons Exiting the
European Union Committee.

Jack, S. (2018). *Jaguar Land Rover Boss: Brexit
threatens £80bn UK investment*. BBC website. Accessed
July 5. Retrieved from https://www.bbc.co.uk/news/
business-44719656

Lamb, M. (2018). Powered by people and technology, the
owner managed business view in 2018. *Moore Stephens*,
February.

Manning, J. (2018). Nissan has been left 'in the dark' on
Brexit and warns of slow decline. *Chronicle Live*, June 28.

Nielsen, B. (2017, September). *Countdown to Brexit; Interim Report produced for Productivity & Skills Commission West Midlands Combined Authority*. Institute for Design & Economic Acceleration (IDEA), Birmingham City University.

OBR. (2018, October). *Brexit and the OBR's forecasts*. Discussion Paper No 3.

O'Carroll, L. (2018). BMW will shut UK sites if customs delays clog supply post-Brexit. *The Guardian*. Accessed 25th June. Retrieved from https://www.theguardian.com/business/2018/jun/25/bmw-will-shut-uk-sites-if-customs-delays-clog-supply-post-brexit

O'Carroll, L., & Topham, G. (2018, June 26). Brexit uncertainty puts thousands of jobs at risk, car industry warns. *The Guardian*.

Office for National Statistics. (2017). *Regional gross value added (balanced), UK: 1998 to 2016*. Retrieved from https://www.ons.gov.uk/economy/grossvalueaddedgva/bulletins/regionalgrossvalueaddedbalanceduk/1998to2016

Office for National Statistics. (2018). Gross Domestic Product: Year on Year growth: CVM SA %. Retrieved from https://www.ons.gov.uk/economy/grossdomesticproductgdp/timeseries/ihyp/pn2.

Owen, J. (2018). *For UK business, the EU is the best place to look for advice on Brexit preparations*. London: Institute for Government.

Percival, M., & Barrett, T. (2018). *Open and controlled: A new approach to immigration after Brexit*. London: CBI.

PricewaterhouseCoopers. (2018). UK economic outlook: Prospects for the housing market and the impact of AI on jobs. Retrieved from https://www.pwc.co.uk/services/economics-policy/insights/uk-economic-outlook.html.

Rhodes, C. (2017, December), *Business statistics*. Briefing Paper No. 06152, House of Commons Library, London.

Scottish Government (2018). Preparing Business for Brexit, website accessed 8th June. Retrieved from https://news.gov.scot/news/preparing-business-for-brexit.

Smith, D. (2018). A deal by Christmas, even that's too late, *Sunday Times*, October 7.

Stewart, I., De Senior, D., Porter, R., & Simmons, T. (2018). *The Deloitte CFO survey*. Deloitte, Quarter 3.

Watts, J. (2018). Brexit: Ford warns UK it will take 'whatever action is required after profits hit'. *The Independent website*. Accessed August 19. Retrieved from https://www.independent.co.uk/news/uk/politics/brexit-ford-car-warning-uk-politicians-take-action-protect-business-leave-eu-a8498131.html

# 9

# BREXIT AND THE AUTO INDUSTRY: UNDERSTANDING THE ISSUES FOR SUPPLY CHAIN MANAGEMENT

*Di Li, Shishank Shishank, Alex de Ruyter, Syed Ali, David Bailey, David Hearne and Sukhwinder Salh*

## INTRODUCTION

Globalisation has resulted in high interdependence amongst nations, having been driven by FDI, technological development and market liberalisation. This has seen global value chains lengthening and deepening, leading to not only increased efficiency but also greater fragility with domestic economies becoming sensitive to disruptions in transnational supply chains (Rosecrance et al., 1977). For the UK automotive sector, these developments have gone hand-in-hand with the development of the EU Single Market. Access to the Single Market is crucial for UK businesses: UK exports to the EU were equivalent to 15% of GDP (Ottaviano, Pessoa,

Sampson, & van Reenen, 2014). Crafts (2016) argues that EU membership has increased UK GDP per capita by 8.6% to 10.6%, whilst others put the figure at an astonishing 23.7% (Campos & Coricelli, 2017). Whilst these figures are highly uncertain,[1] it is incontrovertible that the high level of integration of member states has resulted in businesses becoming heavily reliant on access to the Single Market due to the complexity of European supply chains.

In this context, the decision of the UK to leave the EU on 29 March 2019 (at the time of writing) has generated a high degree of uncertainly and anxiety by UK-based manufacturers. The automotive industry has been particularly vocal in this regard, with companies such as Jaguar Land Rover, BMW and Honda warning of the threats to their continued viability to manufacture in the UK in the event of a hard Brexit (BEIS, 2018).

As such, the importance of the automotive industry to the UK economy is evident in that in 2017, the sector was directly worth £15.2 billion to the UK economy and represented over 8% of total UK manufacturing (Brown and Rhodes, 2018). Indeed, the UK is a major global manufacturer in the automotive industry when compared with total world production, being the 13th largest producer of automobiles by volume in the world and the fourth largest within Europe producing over 1.8 million vehicles, of which 1.72 million were cars (SMMT, 2017). UK production was equivalent to £53.9 billion (or 14.7% of total value) in the European industry in 2014 (MarketLine, 2015). In terms of employment, the industry is a major employer in UK manufacturing, with 161,000 people employed in the broader motor vehicle manufacturing sector; equivalent to 6.7% of total manufacturing industry employment and 0.5% of total UK employment (ONS, 2017). In turn, it has been argued that UK workforce itself is a major factor that has promoted the success of the industry, in particular the flexibility the UK provides employers to meet changes in requirements and environment (Automotive Council, 2013).

However, the EU remains the single-largest destination for UK manufactured vehicles, accounting for approximately 50% of UK vehicle exports, with the rest of the world combined accounting for only 30% (Bailey & De Propris, 2017). It is thus this situation, whereby the UK has served to provide a relatively flexible market environment for the sector within the EU, serving as a platform for production extending deep into Europe; that the prospect of Brexit poses considerable challenges for an industry dominated by Just-in-Time (Lean) production techniques. In the sections that follow, we first consider how companies make supply-chain decisions in the sector, before turning to recent developments in the sector in the wake of the Brexit vote (Hearne & De Ruyter, 2018). We then introduce the findings of our own research on interviewing senior managers in the automotive industry in the UK who have some 'ownership' of the issues raised by Brexit, before concluding with implications for supply chain management (SCM).

## BREXIT AND THE SUPPLY CHAIN: KEY ISSUES FOR ANALYSIS

As noted above, within discussions regarding the status of the UK automotive industry, the probable impact of Brexit on supply chains has assumed particular urgency for analysis by academics and practitioners alike. Based on prior extant research, two key sectors where supply chain implications have been considered are agriculture and manufacturing. It has been argued that Brexit could result in the labour costs of the agricultural sector increasing, which would entail challenges for cost reduction (Carson, 2018). For manufacturing industries, the likely impact of Brexit is also that costs would increase. In addition, Brexit could also adversely affect the accuracy (and increase the difficulties) of demand forecasting (Safonovs & Upadhyay, 2017). However, the impact of Brexit on supply chain is still at an early stage – as of course, at the time of writing, Brexit had not actually happened yet. Therefore, in the context of this chapter, we refer instead to the *exposure* of supply chains to Brexit developments and what *scenario planning* companies are undertaking (if any).

It is therefore possible to 'pre-predict' the key issues that might be brought by Brexit (i.e. a 'hard' Brexit), which could potentially affect any industry. One of key issues is rising costs. This could occur directly due to Brexit in the form of customs and excise duties if the UK exits the Single Market and EU Customs Union (Cumming & Zahra, 2016; Vandenbussche et al., 2017). Another potential impact of Brexit could be on human resources. EU skilled workers currently working in the UK could return to the EU should Freedom of Movement be rescinded – which in turn could exacerbate skills shortages in key sectors (Vandenbussche et al., 2017; Salh, Nyfoudi, & De Ruyter, 2017). In addition, some companies could close down UK branches due to shrinkage of the market, or could even relocate their plants or/and R&D centre to other (EU) countries. Finally, inbound foreign direct investment (FDI) to the UK could also decrease, due to the loss of Single Market membership (Bailey & de Propris, 2017; Baldwin, 2016; Dhingra, Ottaviano, Sampson, & Van Reenen, 2016).

In response to the potential impacts of Brexit identified above, conventional approaches to reinforcing the supply chain have been to emphasise increased resilience. As such, it is argued that enhancing supply chain integration could help to build up a higher resilient capability. With information sharing, the 'bullwhip effect' – defined as the distortion of demand information as one moves upstream in the supply chain, causing severe inefficiencies within the whole supply chain (Costantino, Di Gravio,

Shaban, & Tronci, 2013) – could be minimalised and companies would be able to make proper responses to different situations with enough evidence as support.

In addition to integration, it has been argued that Lean implementation could be another approach to enhance resilience. However, there are some arguments from industries which claimed that Brexit could 'sabotage' the extant manufacturing JIT systems that are based on suppliers from the EU (Holden, 2018). However, this does not necessarily mean that Lean implementation should be stopped. When mentioning Lean, many people will equate it to 'reducing cost' or being 'cheap'. In fact, the term 'Lean' actually refers to 'a series of activities or solutions to eliminate waste, reduce non-value added (NVA) operations, and improve … value added (VA)' (Wee & Wu, 2009). Therefore, it is more apposite to interpret 'Lean' as aiming to be more effective and efficient, which arguably is exactly what companies need in order to cope with Brexit-induced uncertainty.

An alternative approach to enhance supply chain resilience could be via that of supply chain segmentation (Safonovs & Upadhyay, 2017). Supply chain segmentation refers to segmented supply chains with a different supply chain strategy for different products with different levels of demand (Godsell, Diefenbach, Clemmow, Towill, & Christopher, 2011). This bespoke approach suggests that it is possible to design more precise strategies for various products which could reduce costs and increase flexibility.

Alternatively, additional costs arising from Brexit could result in supplier re-evaluation, as firms seek to optimise existing supply chains and hence prepare for the supplier 'earthquake' that could be brought about by Brexit. When re-evaluating current suppliers, the total cost of ownership (TCO) could be one update-to-date principle to help companies in choosing between suppliers. Some suppliers might be able to provide a lower price. However, if they are far away from the UK, then lengthy transportation times and low flexibility of changes could result in additional costs. Therefore, if considering TCO, then local suppliers might be able to provide a cheaper total cost, even if their costs of production are higher. As such, a TCO approach might result in companies seeking to 're-shore' operations to the UK in the event of a hard Brexit. Godsell et al. (2017) suggest that this is a distinct possibility, as re-shoring could be a weapon to protect companies from the negative impacts of Brexit.

Finally, new technology development and implementation could be another approach whereby companies could build up a long-term sustainable and stable supply chain which would be less exposed to an unfavourable external environment. For example, 3D printing technology, a feature of 'Industry 4.0', could provide an innovative approach to production – which has been widely used in aerospace industry (Joshi & Sheikh, 2015). 3D printing could also help to enhance the vertical integration of production, as a result, the tiers of suppliers could be reduced (Berman, 2012). Hence, supply chains could become simpler thereby enhancing the capability against urgent change of external environment.

However, this discussion pre-supposes that companies are actively evaluating their supply chain options and considering likely post-Brexit trade scenarios. Indeed, it is widely assumed – particularly in UK Government circles that companies *are* preparing for Brexit as part of normal risk management and contingency planning exercises. However, it is equally possible that (resource-constrained) companies could find that acting in the face of 'unknown unknowns' arising from Brexit is problematic, due to the inability to assign probabilities to unquantifiable scenarios. It is perhaps this that has seen the continued calls from businesses and peak organisations such as the British Chambers of Commerce, for 'clarity' by the UK Government to negotiating an exit from the EU. Hence, in the sections that follow, we seek to evaluate the SCM strategies of firms in the automotive sectors, by specifically asking the following research questions:

- What is the potential impact of Brexit on operation and supply chains?
- Are companies undertaking measures to be 'prepared' for Brexit?
- What mitigating strategies, if any, do they have in place?

## METHODOLOGY

Given the focus of the study on the automotive sector, a case study research strategy was adopted consisting of a mixed-methods research approach (interviews and desktop analysis), underpinned by a pragmatist research philosophy (Morgan, 2014). Semi-structured interviews of approximately 30 minutes to an hour's duration were conducted between June and September 2018 with nine senior managers in automotive firms based predominantly in the West Midlands of the UK. These individuals consisted of a mix of functional areas (procurement, operations, finance, etc.) but the key criterion for interview selection was that these people in some sense 'owned' the issue of Brexit in their organisation. The interview questions covered five themes related to the perceived potential impact of Brexit on the company respondents worked for: SCM; purchasing; legal and compliance; human resources, and; customer service and communications.

Within these envelopes, the aim of the interviews was to understand to what extent managers across these functional areas understood the exposure of their sector to Brexit, what range of options were available in terms of adjusting their business model and what strategies – if any – they had in place to try and mitigate the potential impact of different Brexit scenarios (i.e. hard Brexit with new visa requirements and trade barriers, or soft Brexit). Interview participants were provided with prior information about the purposes of the research so as to ensure fully informed consent, and the interviews were conducted in accordance with the strict ethical tenets of voluntary participation, anonymity, confidentiality and non-disclosure where requested. The interviews were recorded on digital recording software and transcribed using the services of a professional transcription firm. Data were kept on secure services and all name and subject identifiers were destroyed upon the conclusion of the research.

In the sections that follow, we detail the findings of the research in accordance with the themes denoted above. Given the relatively small size of the interview sample, the findings should be considered as indicative rather than necessarily representative, so some degree of caution is necessary in terms of generalising the findings. Due to space limitations, we confine our discussion in this chapter to issues related to purchasing and SCM in general.

## FINDINGS

### On the Potential Impact of Brexit

The supply chain for a majority of companies within the auto industry is not just a domestic phenomenon; supply chains extend across national boundaries, imposing challenges of globalisation on decision-makers who are responsible for designing the supply chain for existing and new product lines (Meixell & Gargeya, 2005). With this level of integration across international boundaries, Brexit brings waste back into the process with the possibility of new border rules and tariffs on parts as they cross borders before being inserted into cars. In this context, one manager from an automotive OEM referred to Brexit as

> *a disaster for the economy and for the country and for our business. As a company, we are very much UK concentrated in terms of our geographical, manufacturing and other supporting services footprint. But we are very international in our sales outlet. So, for us as a company, we bring in lots of things to the UK, people, parts... other stuff. Make them into cars and then export that. So, we are affected for things on the way in and on the way out.*

A tier 1 supplier to the automotive industry noted that on the 'negative side it's likely to increase the amount of administration and paperwork that's involved in dealing with EU companies whatever the outcome'.

In addition to this one of the tier 1 suppliers was concerned with the idea of stockpiling of products in the UK to mitigate for a Brexit, an aspect that contradicts the attributes associated with the just-in-time philosophy, in adding costs (Chopra & Sodhi, 2004) to the business.

## On Brexit 'Preparedness'

With reference to the preparedness of companies to Brexit, an increasing number of companies appear to be worried about the impact of the UK leaving the EU, but there remains little planning and most businesses are unaware of how to tackle this issue. As noted, businesses continue to call for 'clarity' from the UK Government in its negotiating objectives, despite the fact that the Government has released 'no deal scenario' (a scenario where the UK leaves the EU without any agreement) advice.[2] A manager at tier 1 supplier emphasised that

> *For us, we can understand Brexit at a functional level, but to understand it at an enterprise level means combining ... individual views. And, what one means for the next and what that means for the next and what that means for the next, is very difficult and it's trying to join up the dots and make sure that there aren't contradictions – that's a real operational challenge.*

Another manager at an OEM in the same context mentioned that

> *only last year did it become apparent that ..., time was ticking faster than one would have hoped. And consequently one needed to look at the impacts. I think there was a belief that A) it wouldn't ... happen and B) it would happen in a much subtler form, but obviously that didn't quite occur.*

In contrast, another manager from an OEM confirmed two scenario planning options into which they had invested resources, a 'base scenario' and an 'alternative scenario'. The base scenario was that of a Canada–EU style free trade agreement; that is, that the UK would leave the EU, leave the Single Market, leave the customs union and freedom of movement with EU countries would end. As such, the Jurisdiction of the Court of Justice of the European Union would end pretty much in line with the UK Government's 'red lines' but that the UK would negotiate a tariff free trade agreement with the EU. The alternative scenario that was considered was exactly the same, except there would be tariffs; so, a WTO-style scenario.

Although this company looked at and considered the likelihood that all the different models that exist, so the Norway model, the Switzerland model, the Ukraine model, the Turkey model, the Canada model, WTO model may be applicable. But the company believes that based on prudent and probabilistic assessment of scenarios, either of the two; a Canada–EU style agreement, or default to WTO trade conventions might be the most likely outcome. Although they have invested resources in planning for these two scenarios, they also have worked to make sure that the whole business is using exactly the same set of scenarios. In addition, the company is working on an exercise to consider how they would cope with a no deal outcome. The manager in this context of no deal scenario between the UK and the EU went on to say

> *although my guidance to the business in this is a very low probability scenario, it's **not** zero probability because it's very low probability. We have been exercised to consider it in all seriousness (our emphasis).*

### Mitigating Strategies: Understanding the Supply Chain?

A majority of people are familiar with large UK-based OEM brands such as Jaguar Land Rover, Rolls-Royce and GKN. However, the multitude of suppliers and partners that make these companies' final products possible often go unrecognised (APMG, 2015). This aspect of the supply chain is missed and ignored to the detriment of the UK's entire industrial base. Evidence suggests that the UK Government had been supportive of reshoring production and increasing the scope of the local supply chain. However, this was before the Brexit referendum result in 2016. The concept of onshoring suppliers was one of the options suggested by a manager of an OEM to mitigate the risk of disruption that might be caused in the supply chain.

In light of evidence from the industry, the possibility of reshoring suppliers would mitigate potential tariffs on traded car components. Stojanovic and Rutter (2018) suggest that on finished cars there could be a potential 10% tariff (at WTO thresholds) within the automotive sector, so that finished cars would suffer a 10% tariff in addition to car components' tariffs ranging from 2.5% to 4.5%. However, the sector also depends on intermediate inputs that cross borders many times – and so costs could accumulate in the supply chain. Further to this, the existence of sunk costs in the form of existing contracts with suppliers could also act to limit flexibility to respond quickly to Brexit, with one manager in a tier 1 supplier commenting that they would not change suppliers in the short term. Indeed, in the short term, it could be that companies will simply have to devote additional resources to managing any increased documentation requirements related to rules of origin and diagonal cumulation, so as to ensure (as best as possible) frictionless movement of supplies cross border to avoid delays and stockpiling in order to fulfil current orders.

Hence, in the context of the inevitable lag times to affecting any changes to SCM procedures, the proposed transition period to the end of 2020 (at the time of writing) was regarded with a high degree of scepticism by our respondents. As such, a manager from a tier 1 supplier stated that

> *Okay, so we have a two year transition period agreed. But, our own Government studies show that we need five to ten years to put some sort of system in place. So what do we do for the three to eight years in-between that? Who collects these customs? Who actually does all of this stuff that*

> *we've cooked up? So the practicalities as well as the*
> *legalities I don't ... Really ... Understand ....*

OEMs are also appear to be examining the added costs and the contribution from suppliers in meeting these costs. An issue that will need to be dealt with individual suppliers.

Finally, our research suggests that OEMs might not be fully aware of the lower tiers in their supply chain and the effects of Brexit on suppliers lower down the chain will have an impact on any – or all – of the suppliers in the upper tiers of the supply chain, for example,

> *We have a very strong understanding of who our*
> *suppliers are at Tier 1 and then direct to Tier 2,*
> *and visibility ... that means we worked with that*
> *supplier for the engineering, but we don't own the*
> *commercial relationship, it goes through a Tier 1.*
> *Beyond that, we don't really have much knowledge*
> *of who our suppliers are and where the parts come*
> *from, and therefore, we don't particularly have a*
> *working group at the moment with our suppliers,*
> *it's all kind of like every person for themselves.*

## DISCUSSION

Our findings have highlighted questions of disparity in Brexit readiness levels amongst the OEMs and tier 1 companies whose representatives we interviewed. At one end of the spectrum are companies with no or minimum understanding of readiness to Brexit, whilst on the other are companies that have thought through and may even be prepared to mitigate the impact of Brexit. To reiterate, this disparity amongst the sample might not be generalisable across the population, but is certainly indicative of the work and input required to ensure 'frictionless supply chains' in the advent of a hard Brexit, in managing the complications and obstacles that the UK as a constituent nation in a trade bloc could face after a significant political shift to the status of being a third-party country to the EU.

As such, major OEMs and tier 1 suppliers will need to work much more closely with companies further down their supply chains in order to help them mitigate the risks faced, particularly in terms of timely deliveries. Warehousing might also need to be considered in some scenarios, but this will vary by component and site. Therefore, companies need to have a further understanding of Lean and implement it in a deeper level, for example, apply a lean philosophy on more operations processes rather than just pure manufacturing processes. For example, this could consist of extending lean manufacturing to a lean supply chain. In order to do this, companies need to map their value stream in a deep detail and re-evaluate and optimise by a lean philosophy annually (Wee & Wu, 2009). In this way, business operation processes could become simpler and smoother; presuming higher efficiency, so as to help achieve a lower total cost.

## CONCLUSION

This chapter has explored the potential impacts of Brexit on the automotive sector supply chain. Brexit in the words of industry experts means considerable amount of increase in waste (Lean philosophy), which the automotive industry has tried to reduce over time. The automotive supply chain would incur sudden increased costs, increased inventory costs for both supplies and complete products causing delays (Bailey & De Propris, 2017) and reduced productivity.

It is evident from our study that almost all the automotive companies have no plan to mitigate the challenges which will be brought by Brexit to their supply chain. A few of the companies (specifically OEMs and tier 1 suppliers) with disposable resources have planned and might be ready, but they have not published details of any actions that they might take and as of yet no action has been taken. This could also be due to the fact that companies have not been able to fully identify the threats posed by a hard Brexit (back to our 'unknown unknowns'). Companies agree that there are very little things they can do now, and that the automotive industry is waiting for Government to publish definitive directions.

In addition, companies have considered more local sourcing and reshoring, but might relocate their existing plants as well. This means the supply chain base/network/configuration may be re-mapped post-Brexit. This can also be referred to as opportunities that might arise to be ceased by the companies, such as access to other global markets. It can be confirmed that some companies have dedicated teams to specifically manage Brexit issues. However, our evidence to date suggests that these teams appear not to connect and communicate with the rest of their organisation and are primarily working in a silo, with very little strategic output to direct the focus of their company.

From a company perspective, companies significantly lack understanding of Brexit. In summary, Brexit is unpredictable, uncertain and likely to cause disruption and delays to the automotive supply chains and all of these will be transferred as a financial cost, which could be millions of pounds per hour. Further research is needed to boost our understanding in this regard.

## ACKNOWLEDGMENTS

The authors would like to thank Opentext for their support of this research. In addition, the writing of this chapter has been supported by the EU Horizon 2020 project

MAKERS – Smart Manufacturing for EU Growth and Prosperity, a project funded by the Horizon 2020 Research and Innovation Staff Exchange Programme, under the Marie Sklodowska-Curie Actions, grant agreement number 691192.

## NOTES

1. Coutts, Gudgin, and Buchanan (2018) argue against such an effect at all.

2. UK government Brexit advice, https://www.gov.uk/government/brexit [accessed 16 October 2018].

## REFERENCES

Automotive Council. (2013). *Driving success: A strategy for growth and sustainability in the UK automotive sector*. Retrieved from https://www.gov.uk/government/uploads/system/uploads/attachment_data/file/211901/13-975-driving-success-uk-automotive-strategy-for-growth-and-sustainability.pdf. Accessed on September 25, 2018.

Bailey, D., & De Propris, L. (2017). Brexit and the UK automotive industry. *National Institute Economic Review*, *242*(1), R51–R59.

Berman, B. (2012). 3-D printing: The new industrial revolution. *Business Horizons*, *55*(2), 155–162.

Brown, J. and Rhodes, C. (2018). *The motor industry: statistics and policy*. House of Commons Library. Available at: http://researchbriefings.files.parliament.uk/documents/SN00611/SN00611.pdf [Accessed 04 Feb 2019]

Business Energy and Industrial Strategy Committee (BEIS). (2018). The impact of Brexit on the automotive sector.

Fifth Report of the Business, Energy and Industrial Strategy Committee Session 2017–19, London.

Campos, N., & Coricelli, F. (2017). EU Membership, Mrs Thatcher's reforms and Britain's economic decline. *Comparative Economic Studies*, 59(2), 169–193.

Carson, K. (2018). Agricultural training and the labour productivity challenge. *International Journal of Agricultural Management*, 6(3–4), 131–133.

Chopra, S., & Sodhi, M. S. (2004). Managing risk to avoid supply-chain breakdown. *MIT Sloan Management Review, 2004*, 53–61.

Costantino, F., Di Gravio, G., Shaban, A., & Tronci, M. (2013). Exploring the bullwhip effect and inventory stability in a seasonal supply chain. *International Journal of Engineering Business Management*, 5, 23.

Coutts, K., Gudgin, G., & Buchanan, J. (2018). *How the economics profession got it wrong on Brexit*. Working Paper 493. Centre for Business Research, University of Cambridge.

Crafts, N. (2016). The growth effects of EU membership for the UK: A review of the evidence. *University of Warwick CAGE Working Paper, 280*.

Cumming, D., & Zahra, S. (2016). International business and entrepreneurship implications of Brexit. *British Journal of Management*, 27, 687–692.

Dhingra, S., Ottaviano, G., Sampson, T., & Van Reenen, J. (2016). The impact of Brexit on foreign investment in the UK., *BREXIT, 2016*, 24.

Godsell, J., Diefenbach, T., Clemmow, C., Towill, D., & Christopher, M. (2011). Enabling supply chain segmentation through demand profiling. *International Journal of Physical Distribution & Logistics Management*, 41(3), 296–314.

Godsell, J., Ignatius, J., Karatzas, A., King, J., Li, D., & Moore, J. (2017). *Realities of reshoring: A UK perspective*. Coventry: WMG, University of Warwick.

Hearne, D., & De Ruyter, A. (2018). *Regional success after Brexit: The need for new measures*. Bingley: Emerald Publishing.

Holden, M. (2018, February 6). *Just-in-time: The production system Brexit is set to sabotage*. Retrieved from http://www. politics.co.uk/comment-analysis/2018/02/06/just-in-time-the-production-system-brexit-is-set-to-sabotage. Accessed on April 11, 2018.

Joshi, S., & Sheikh, A. (2015). 3D printing in aerospace and its long-term sustainability. *Virtual and Physical Prototyping*, 10(4), 175–185.

MarketLine. (2015). *Automotive manufacturing in the United Kingdom*. London: MarketLine Industry Profile.

Meixell, M., & Gargeya, V. (2005). Global supply chain design: A literature review and critique. *Transport Research, Part E*(41), 531–550.

Morgan, D. (2014). Pragmatism as a paradigm for social research. *Qualitative Inquiry*, 20(8), 1045–1053.

Office for National Statistics (ONS). (2017). *Business Register and Employment Survey'*. Retrieved from https://www.nomisweb. co.uk/query/construct/summary.asp?mode=construct&version= 0&dataset=189. Accessed on September 26, 2018.

Ottaviano, G.I.P., Pessoa, J.P., Sampson, T., & Van Reenen, J. (2014). *Brexit or Fixit? The trade and welfare effects of leaving the European Union*. Center of

Economic Performance. Available at: http://eprints.lse.ac.uk/57958/1/__lse.ac.uk_storage_LIBRARY_Secondary_libfile_shared_repository_Content_Centre_for_Economic_Performance_Policy%20Analysis_pa016.pdf [Accessed 04 Feb 2019]

Rosecrance, R., Alexandroff, A., Koehler, W., Kroll, J., Laqueur, S., & Stocker, J. (1977). Whither Interdependence? *International Organization*, *31*(3), 425–471.

Safonovs, R., & Upadhyay, A. (2017). Is your Brexit supply chain resilient enough? The British footwear manufacturers' perspective. *Strategic Direction*, *33*(11), 34–36.

Salh, S., Nyfoudi, M., & De Ruyter, A. (2017). Future regulation of the UK workforce. In D. Bailey, and L. Budd (Eds.), *The Political Economy of Brexit*. Newcastle upon Tyne: Agenda Publishing.

Society of Motor Manufacturers and Traders (SMMT). (2017). *SMMT motor industry facts 2017*. London: SMMT. Available at: https://www.smmt.co.uk/wp-content/uploads/sites/2/SMMT-Motor-Industry-Facts-2017_online_May.pdf [Accessed 04 Feb 2019]

Vandenbussche, H., Connell Garcia, W., & Simons, W. (September, 2017). Global value chains, trade shocks and jobs: an application to Brexit. Center for Economic Studies, Ku Leuvan.

Wee, H., & Wu, S. (2009). Lean supply chain and its effect on product cost and quality: A case study on Ford Motor Company. *Supply Chain Management: An International Journal*, *14*(5), 335–41.

# CONCLUSION: WHERE DO WE GO FROM HERE?

*Alex de Ruyter and Beverley Nielsen*

This book has sought to provide an account of the process of Brexit as it unfolds, following the declaration of the intent to leave the European Union (EU) under Article 50 by Theresa May on 29 March 2017. In so doing, one of the key aims of this book has been to provide an informed, evidence-based narrative from both sides of the debate, as to the likely direction of travel in terms of the process (and progress) of negotiations. The book was thus structured into two parts; Part I dealing with the process and progress of negotiations, and possible prospects going forward; whilst Part II sought to ascertain the likely impact of Brexit on key sectors of the economy, namely, financial services (Boleat), and manufacturing (Li et al.; McCabe et al.). Notwithstanding the divergent views presented (from both academics and practitioners), what is evident is that Brexit (particularly a 'hard' Brexit) would entail a protracted period of adjustment for the UK economy (i.e. likely to incur a significant economic cost in the short to medium term; and with potential for longer-term damage given the path-dependent nature of any future trajectory of economic performance).

Going forward, at the time of writing (October 2018), the stance of the UK Government had been essentially to keep the whole of the UK in the EU Customs Union for a 'temporary' period until such a point where other (technological) solutions to the problem of a hard border in Northern Ireland become viable. The proposal would also, in effect, have kept Northern Ireland in the Single Market for goods (subject to approval from a Northern Ireland Assembly that has not sat for over 18 months now), so as to uphold the Good Friday Agreement and adhere to its pledge to protect the all-Ireland economy. Suffice to say, this represented a significant (if not seismic) shift from Theresa May's initial position of 'Brexit means Brexit' – a position elaborated in her February 2017 Lancaster House speech, in which Brexit meant leaving the EU Customs Union, leaving the Single Market and no longer abiding by the jurisdiction of the Court of Justice of the EU.

Not surprisingly, this 'creeping shift' towards more of a Norway-style deal with the EU, rather than a more limited arrangement led to a backlash from pro-Brexit MPs such as the 50-odd Conservative MPs that form the 'European Research Group' (ERG), chaired by Jacob Rees-Mogg. Of course, the government's articulated stance had already led to the Cabinet resignations of prominent Leave referendum campaigners, Boris Johnson and David Davis. As such, for the ERG, the government's proposals risk the UK being kept in a customs union with the EU indefinitely, which would undermine the 'clean' (hard) Brexit they were seeking, whereby the UK would only enter into negotiating a free trade agreement with the EU, plus a number of ad hoc additions. This would, in essence, be similar to the arrangements that Canada has with the EU with additional bolt-ons. Equally, for the Democratic Unionist Party (DUP), the proposals added to their fears that NI in effect would diverge away from the rest of the UK.

This raises the somewhat problematic issue of trying to offer insights as to what we think the likely thrust of Brexit developments will be – assuming of course, that Brexit is carried out and that some circumstance preventing this, such as a 'remain' vote in another referendum, does not come to pass – not improbable at the time of writing, although this would not be without its difficulties. Referenda are usually binary, and for good reason. Those which give multiple choices are potentially subject to the *Condorcet paradox*.[1] In all probability, therefore, another referendum could be faced with a difficult situation in which a majority of voters still wish to leave the EU, as per the 2016 referendum, but do not generate a clear majority in terms of what kind of Brexit they want. As such, the prospect of 'no deal' (even should the UK secure a transition period) also at the time of writing also remains a distinct possibility.

A no-deal scenario could have enormous effects, were the UK to suddenly leave the European Aviation Safety Agency, European Medicines Agency, European Chemicals Agency and other similar bodies. Cross-border broadcasting (see our blog on this here) would be immediately in jeopardy and the haulage sector would face severe problems as the UK defaulted to pre-EU arrangements (the 1968 Vienna Convention and European Convention of Ministers of Transport). Furthermore, the UK will need to put into place open-skies arrangements with all its global counterparts to keep aircraft flying and it will lose access to all those free trade agreements it currently enjoys as an EU member (including with Turkey, Mexico, South Korea and many others). While the prospect of aircraft being grounded remains remote, there is a real possibility of other partners playing hardball (as the example of the US has shown) without the backing of the entire EU behind it. In any event, a sudden 'no deal' exit would trigger a significant economic shock and would greatly increase the risk of a recession.

Our task is therefore to outline some key issues going forward, regardless of the outcome of Brexit negotiations, or otherwise of the UK Government returning to 'the People' to determine the nature of the Brexit endpoint via another referendum. In the remainder of the book, we provisionally explore these under the following themes:

(1) *Identity and the future of the 'United' Kingdom.* Much has been made about the vote to the Leave the UK as being an expression of the desire of people to reassert national sovereignty (leaving aside for now, the problematic nature of sovereignty in a globalised word). This has been a view articulated by prominent Brexiteer politicians, such as Boris Johnson, who in trying to argue for a 'liberal' Brexit (a la John Stuart Mill), evoked the notion that law-making could only be legitimately undertaken by 'the people' as a 'demos'. For Johnson, this 'demos' is embodied in the UK as an organic nation-state (and hence that the EU lacks legitimacy in this regard). Hence, 'only the nation can legitimate' obedience to laws[2] and Brexit represents as reassertion of the primacy of 'Britons' as the demos to undertake this. It is thus of some pertinence to explore notions of 'Britishness' and see how pervasive they are in the UK at large, today.

In this regard, the 2011 Census (data available for England and Wales) provides data on ethnicity and identity. What is striking here, in contrast to Johnson's purported Demos above, is that those who self-identify as 'British' (either to the exclusion of any other identity or in concert with another) now number a minority in the UK, with only 29% of respondents in England identifying themselves as British. In contrast, 70% identified themselves as 'English'[3]. The divergence between London and the rest of England is also starkly apparent – and only in London did 'Britishness' compete with 'Englishness' as an identity; with 38% of respondents identifying as British, and 44% English (notably, given the cosmopolitan nature of London, 'other' identities comprised 26%). The 2014 Scottish independence referendum also illustrated this divergence in a very dramatic fashion, with 45% of voters desiring to break away from the UK (De Ruyter & Hearne, 2018). In turn, an increasing sense of Englishness in England has also been accompanied by increasing resentment against the 1997 devolution settlement offered to Scotland (Jones, Lodge, Henderson, & Wincott, 2012). This was epitomised in the famous 'West Lothian Question' (Bogdanor, 2010), whereby Scottish MPs could vote on English affairs, but not vice versa, which prompted the Cameron Government to explore the prospect of 'English votes for English laws' (Hayton, 2015) in the aftermath of the Scottish independence referendum.

Thus, not surprisingly, these fault-lines between London, Scotland and the rest of the UK manifested in the Brexit vote (and for which the prior growth of 'Englishness' could have been seen as a portent thereof), which was characterised by strong variations between the constituent 'nations' of the UK, with Scotland and Northern Ireland in particular demonstrating a strong Remain vote share, alongside London. Thus it could be argued that the Brexit vote represents the reassertion of an English identity or Demos, rather than a British one, and thus that the UK is no more of an organic (or legitimate) political entity than the EU. Hearne and De Ruyter (2018), writing in this vein argue that:

> *the logical corollary of Johnson's argument is that the UK should be scrapped in favour of separate states for different nations [Demos]. Where that would leave the 25% of the population who do identify as British remains to be seen.*[4]

Indeed, post-referendum, there is an impasse (at the time of writing) over the status of the Northern Ireland border and Scottish (and Welsh) government dissatisfaction over perceived lack of consultation by the UK Government: that is, of the 'uncertainty surrounding... constitutional voice for the devolved institutions in Scotland and elsewhere' (McHarg &

Mitchell, 2017). This in turn adds further impetus to the arguments of those who demand reunification on the island of Ireland, or of Scottish independence. Examined in this light, should Brexit come to pass, the future of the UK in surviving as a coherent political entity looks bleak. Such predictions are not new, with Tom Nairn (1977) having first penned *The Break-up of Britain* over 40 years ago. However, Brexit, with the seemingly intractable constitutional issues generated in its wake, has given them renewed vigour (and added a renewed validity to Nairn's arguments). As such, (Budd, 2018), considering the likely economic shock to Northern Ireland from a hard Brexit, argued that:

> *its future may lie in an All-Ireland solution.*
> *Ironically, the Conservative and Unionist*
> *government and its current support from the*
> *Democratic Unionist Party may create the*
> *conditions for a united Ireland and consequently*
> *the break-up on the union of the UK.*[5]

If nothing else, this calls for an urgent, fundamental revisit to the debate as to the nature of the UK, and what form the 'demos' within it (and consequent governance structures) should take, post-Brexit. As such, one could argue that nations are only one form of identity and, moreover, these identities are frequently changeable over time (Anderson, 1983; Hearne & De Ruyter, 2018).

(2) Economic 'sovereignty'. In this final section, we consider some attendant implications of the Brexit vote as being a desire to restore 'sovereignty' over decision-making on matters that affect the UK. This was a theme that occurred repeatedly throughout the period leading up to the June 2016 referendum, and up to the present day (at the time of writing). Sovereignty, of course, has many dimensions, but for some, this could be interpreted solely in terms of the UK setting

immigration policy, free from the strictures of 'Freedom of Movement' in the EU Single Market, for example.

Of course, any such discussion has to start off from the UK's *actual* decision-making position within the EU at the time of writing, rather than some imagined one. The notion that the UK lacked decision-making ability within the confines of EU membership was a sentiment that was expressed widely during the Centre for Brexit Studies roadshow series of public engagement focus groups in Leave-voting communities. This was also evident in European polling data (TNS Opinion & Social, 2015), suggesting that UK nationals felt unusually disempowered with respect to institutions of the EU. However, on a practical level, the UK Government has been an integral member of the European Council. As such, the elected representatives of the UK have had a major role in European policymaking – and by dint of the UK's size, this is far larger than the vast majority of European states. In addition, the majority of European laws are adopted under the 'ordinary legislative procedure', which gives the European Parliament and the Council an equal right to reject or amend laws. UK nationals, naturally, have had the right to vote for members of this parliament in regular elections and therefore have had every bit as much influence on European legislation as the average German, Italian or Spaniard (Hearne & De Ruyter, 2018).

Exiting the EU (as we have seen within the bounds of this book), it is claimed that the UK will be 'free' to pursue its own trade deals, at terms it sees fit. This is what Secretary of State for International Trade, Liam Fox, described in February 2018 as 'multi-country alliances of the *like-minded* right down to bilateral arrangements'[6] (our emphasis), in addition to his previously noted comments in our introduction to this book about 'deregulating' the UK labour market. We opened this book by arguing that the Brexiteer perspective essentially was one of further deregulation towards the US model. In practice, however, the UK's ability to influence the content of trade agreements with principle trading partners outside of the EU – that is, the US and China, will be limited, given the disproportionate imbalance in bargaining power between the UK as a mid-sized economy and these two economic superpowers.

In addition, the governance mechanisms used in trade deals including the US (e.g. North American Free Trade Agreement [NAFTA]) are also more opaque than the EU, involving as they do the use of Investor-State Dispute Settlement Procedures that can result in companies suing governments deemed to engage in anti-competitive behaviour. Under these arrangements, such private panels can (and do) overturn the decisions of sovereign governments (Jarman, 2014). The question thus may be asked, just what is economic 'sovereignty' for a mid-sized economy such as the UK, seeking to strike trade deals with the US, or China, or India, or even Australia or Peru for that matter? The simple answer is, far less than that it has currently enjoyed under the shared sovereignty arrangements underpinning its period of EU membership. A more nuanced response might also consider that in today's globalised world, economic 'sovereignty' for the individual nation-state can only ever be partial, as all trade agreements involve a trade-off of sovereignty (even more so for smaller and mid-sized open economies).

In practice, the most likely scenario is that the UK – assuming that it can survive as a political entity – will be a rule-taker, rather than a rule-maker (or even co-creator). As such, it will either stay within the European regulatory orbit, or otherwise drift into the American one (we may largely disregard the Chinese one due to reasons of relative geographic proximity and cultural norms). In neither of these cases (in contrast to some of the views expressed in these pages, we would argue), will the expectations of those who voted to leave the EU be upheld. It now remains to be seen how the concluding phases of Brexit unfold.

## NOTES

1. The Condorcet paradox demonstrates that social choices can violate transitivity. Imagine a world in which voters have three choices: A, B and C. One-third of voters prefer A to B and B to C (A>B>C). One-third of voters prefer B>C>A, and the final third of voters prefer C>A>B. Whatever choice is eventually made (A, B or C), two-thirds of voters can be made happier by choosing a different outcome. For example, if A is chosen, both the second and third group of voters (i.e. 66.7%) would prefer C. The same is true for all others. Even worse, Arrow's Impossibility Theorem demonstrates that, under sensible conditions it is impossible to solve this dilemma without some individual being able in effect to 'dictate' the social ranking – in other words a form of dictatorship.

2. Boris Johnson (2018). '*Uniting for a Great Brexit*' Foreign Secretary's Speech. Policy Exchange.

3. https://www.ons.gov.uk/peoplepopulationandcommunity/culturalidentity/ethnicity/articles/ethnicityandnationalidentityinengland andwales/2012-12-11#national-identity-in-england-and-wales Accessed on 20 October 2018.

4. https://centreforbrexitstudiesblog.wordpress.com/2018/02/16/boris-stuart-johnson-on-liberty/#_ENREF_5 Accessed on 18 October 2018.

5. https://centreforbrexitstudiesblog.wordpress.com/2018/06/08/northern-irelands-dance-to-the-music-of-time-of-brexit/ Accessed on 19 October 2018.

6. https://news.sky.com/story/globetrotter-liam-fox-to-slam-jeremy-corbyns-customs-union-bid-11269242 Accessed on 21 October 2018.

## REFERENCES

Anderson, B. (1983). *Imagined communities: Reflections on the origin and spread of nationalism*. London: Verso.

Bogdanor, V. (2010). The West Lothian question. *Parliamentary Affairs*, 63(1), 156–172.

Budd, L. (2018). Northern Ireland's Dance to the Music of Time of Brexit. [Blog post] Retrieved from

https://centreforbrexitstudiesblog.wordpress.com/2018/06/08/
northern-irelands-dance-to-the-music-of-time-of-brexit/

De Ruyter, A., & Hearne, D. (2018). [Blog post] Brexit and
the call for a second referendum. Retrieved from: https://
centreforbrexitstudiesblog.wordpress.com/2018/07/10/
brexit-and-the-call-for-a-second-referendum/

Hayton, R. (2015). The coalition and the politics of the
English question. *The Political Quarterly*, *86*(1), 125–132.

Hearne, D., & De Ruyter, A. (2018). Boris "Stuart"
Johnson on Liberty. [Blog post] Retrieved from https://
centreforbrexitstudiesblog.wordpress.com/2018/02/16/
boris-stuart-johnson-on-liberty/

Jarman, H. (2014). Public health and the transatlantic trade
and investment partnership. Editorial. *European Journal of
Public Health*, *24*(2), 181.

Jones, R. W., Lodge, G., Henderson, A., & Wincott, D.
(2012). *The dog that finally barked: England as an emerging
political community*. Report: Institute for Public Policy
Research. Retrieved from https://www.ippr.org/publications/
the-dog-that-finally-barked-england-as-an-emerging-
political-community. Accessed on 3 October 2018.

McHarg, A., & Mitchell, J. (2017). Brexit and Scotland. *The
British Journal of Politics and International Relations*, *19*(3),
512–526.

Nairn, T. (1977). *The break-up of Britain: Crisis and
neo-nationalism* (1st ed.). London: New Left Books.

TNS Opinion & Social. (2015) *Public Opinion in the
European Union*. Brussels: European Commission. Standard
Eurobarometer 83 - Spring 2015. DOI: 10.2775/734143

# INDEX